CREATIVE CANVAS
EMBROIDERY

CREATIVE CANVAS
EMBROIDERY

A Stitch by Stitch
Guide to Needlepoint

EFFIE MITROFANIS

BLANDFORD

A BLANDFORD BOOK

First published in the UK 1991
by Blandford
(a Cassell imprint)
Villiers House
41/47 Strand
LONDON
WC2N 5JE

First published in Australia in 1990 by
Simon & Schuster Australia

Designed and produced for the publisher
by J.M. McGregor Pty Ltd, PO Box 6990,
Gold Coast Mail Centre, Qld. 4217

British Library Cataloguing in Publication Data

Mitrofanis, Effie.
Creative canvas embroidery: a stitch by stitch guide to needlepoint.

1. Canvas embroidery.
I. Title.

746.442

ISBN 0-7137-2240-1

Diagrams by Anna Warren
Design by Anna Warren
Photography by Michael Simmons

Typeset in Hanover by Post Typesetters, Brisbane
Printed in Hong Kong by South China Printing Co (1988) Ltd

CONTENTS

INTRODUCTION

What to Expect

*T*he aim of this book is to teach a basic and comprehensive study of canvas work stitchery, or needle point. By the time you've worked through the book, you will have begun to master the techniques of canvas embroidery, including an understanding of simple design.

But, above all, this book concentrates on creative applications of stitchery and design — and all the fun that can be had in the process! I take great pleasure in hunting down threads that are just the right colour. And I've met some of the most interesting people when we've discovered at a thread shop counter that we have a common interest. My family and friends are always following up on my latest projects, guessing at what the result might be.

The first step is to master the 'vocabulary' of stitchery — that is, to learn and feel comfortable doing the variety of basic stitches. This can only be achieved by practice and by doing projects. Then the application of what you've learned begins, and the chance not only to acquire some basic design knowledge, but to create and form your own style.

During the six years I've been teaching canvas embroidery the ages of my students have ranged from nine years to eighty-three. Both beginners and experienced embroiderers too often begin with little confidence in their ability to be 'creative'. Yet I am sure that no matter how imaginative, lively, original, inventive, ingenious or resourceful a piece of 'creative embroidery' may be, there is always one essential ingredient: technique. It is through a properly learned and practised technique that one begins to embroider creatively. My aim in this book is, first of all, to teach technique.

I then encourage you to use this technique in your own individual manner — a style unique to you and producing very individual results. Don't be afraid to try something new, or to be inspired by someone else's embroidery. Design is looking, choosing and organising. The combination of technique with your interpretation of the world and influences around you is what makes an individual style that is all your own. Indeed, look at all artists' creations (think of the relationship between 'creative' and 'creation'), be it a garment of clothing, a cake or an embroidery wall hanging. Look at paintings, ceramics, enamelling, jewellery, pottery and textiles for inspiration. Most embroiderers are inspired by another's work and in an endeavour to emulate, create something which is unique by using a different thread, or changing the scale or colour.

Join an embroidery group or gather a few interested friends and acquaintances together (even the lady or gentleman you met at the thread counter). Regular meetings will encourage you to set goals so you'll have something to show off at the next meeting. The stimulation of voicing your ideas and bouncing them off one another will keep you all moving ahead, as well as make it a lot of fun. My family gets a kick out of the good recipes and jokes I come home with after an 'embroidery' meeting!

Go to as many exhibitions and displays as you can to keep in touch with the new ideas that are always happening in the world of art and decoration.

A Brief History

Until the 1970s most innovation in embroidery technique came from Great Britain and the United States. Painted canvas designs — that is, designs copied from famous paintings — were very popular and commercially successful until the mid eighties. Then came a form of American-style 'quick point' (or 'Gros Point') where long straight stitches (5 to 6 in. or 12–15 cm long) created attractive scenes and could be completed very quickly.

At the same time embroiderers in love with embroidery for its own sake were using dozens of canvas work stitches that necessitated a counted thread canvas base. These people have an inexhaustive appetite for new threads, beads, buttons, coral, pieces of bark, seed pods and anything else which can be incorporated into embroidery.

Traditionally devotees of canvas work have liked working on the grid because of the geometric orderliness such organisation gives to the stitches. However, modern-day canvas embroiderers are not satisfied with the flat, symmetrical pattern of traditional stitchery, or the monotony of a tent-stitch-framed 'painting'. They have let their hair down and ignored the grid, covered the canvas with raised, padded and appliquéd areas, overlooked crewel and tapestry threads, combined new and varied threads in one needle, and added 'foreign objects' such as beads, glass, sequins, seed pods, feathers and bark to create a textural statement or feeling about a favourite subject. Subjects vary greatly, from plant life, landscapes and all forms of nature including embroidered interpretations of bark, rocks, birds, trees, sea and shore and microscopic life, to architecture and urban life. The possibilities are endless.

Instead of limiting canvas embroidery to a set of rigid rules and guidelines, the aim is to explore other techniques for a richer, more raised and textured effect. Works incorporate surface stitchery, needleweaving, appliqué, quilting, cut work, patchwork, weaving and three dimensional forms. Tassels, cords, ribbons and ruching are added to the finished product.

Canvas embroidery is indebted to English teachers of embroidery who have put out so many books on design, colour and technique since 1960. These served to whet embroiderers' appetites and enrich their palette. Designers from America have also had a great influence.

Finally, realizing and incorporating the many ethnic groups and backgrounds within any culture will produce designs and embroidery unique to each individual character and setting. That sort of expression is really what it's all about.

And the getting there is what we're *now* about...

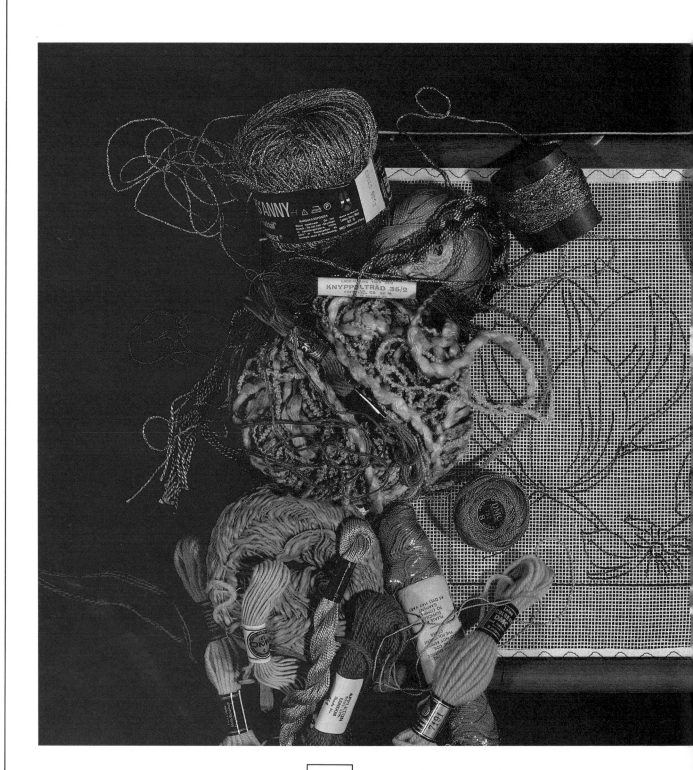

1

GETTING READY
TO GET STARTED:
MATERIALS AND EQUIPMENT

One of the most important things to remember when setting out is that there is no need to spend great quantities of money on material and equipment. Initially you will only need to buy a selection of six to ten wools, threads and yarns, some canvas material and a frame. You can even avoid buying a frame since it is quite easy to make one (as I have had to do when funds were low). Alternatively, a wooden hoop may be used.

Wools, Threads and Yarns

To obtain the best effect a range of different wools, threads and yarns is desirable. Unless you are interpreting a specific design with pre-determined colours, I suggest that you buy a range of different tones of one colour. Dark, medium and light tones, plus cream, bone, off-white and other neutrals. If you wish to combine another colour, again choose several shades of a harmonious or contrasting colour. For example soft pinks or apricots could be contrasted with soft brown, cream and off-white. Or you might mix and match soft greens, cream, pink *or* yellow, off-white and neutrals. Choose colours that please you and that you are happy working with — these are your intuitive colours and we achieve our best results when working with colours with which we are compatible.

Selections of threads can be compiled from knitting wools, knitting cotton, bubbly cotton, crewel wool, tapestry wool, coton perle (numbers 3, 5 and 8), stranded cotton, *coton a broder* and crochet cotton. Most of these wools, yarns and cottons are readily available at department stores, craft and wool shops.

Choose a thickness of thread to correspond with the stitch as well as the size of the canvas you have chosen. Some stitches cover the canvas more than others. If the stitch is unable to be recognised because of thread buildup, change to a thinner thread.

For example: you are using a tapestry wool or 8-ply knitting yarn and the thread is building up until it looks like an unre-cognisable knot. Change the yarn to a 5-ply knitting wool or something of equal weight in crochet or embroidery thread. If the 5-ply knitting or crochet thread is too thick, change to a 4-ply fine knitting yarn, crochet cotton or any other thread of equal or suitable thickness. Some wools can be split and used where a finer thread is required.

Sometimes it is desirable to use a thinner thread in order to show the stitch to its best advantage (even if the canvas shows through). This choice is up to the individual embroiderer to aim for the result you are happy with or the goal you are trying to achieve. This is all a matter of taste. Eyelet, ray or fan stitches require particular care when choosing thread as many stitches have to go into one hole and can cause a big build up of thread. It is best to choose a relatively thin thread for these types of stitches. The only sure way of deciding the best result is for you to try different threads and discover by experimentation, preferably on a spare piece of canvas. (See Chapter 3 on The Sampler.)

Crewel wool is pleasant to use and control, being very soft to the touch and thereby easy on the hands. There is a large range of colours available from selected suppliers. However, when choosing colours in crewel wools be careful that they are not too lifeless, muted or toned down as the overall effect can be unexpectedly boring. It is my experience that most embroiderers who buy crewel wool use it for cushions, panels, seat covers, fire screens and such household decorations requir-ing a muted or subdued 'olde worlde', antique appearance. Therefore when choosing crewel wool colours for use in your creative embroidery ensure that you combine purer colours of knitting wools and cottons with the crewel wool to achieve a balance of bright and subdued colours. The same awareness should be observed when choosing tapestry wools, although in recent years the colours of tapestry wools have brightened and the range has enlarged.

In my experience, I've seen many beginners using only hanks of tapestry wools left over from picture kits. The product is often a dark, dull, mono-tone result unbroken by bright knitting wools, boucles, shiny cotton, silks or metal thread. If you do have a stash of old yarns inherited from your grandmother or next door neighbour by all means use them! But select carefully *from* these rather than designing your creative embroidery around the threads you have inherited. If a beginner limits herself from the start by using an uninspiring bag of leftovers for the sake of economy, the result will reflect just that. Although you needn't spend lots of money laying in an enormous array of colours and types of thread, a few well-chosen ones are very important.

Half the fun of embroidery is choosing and selecting thread, eventually building up a collection that not only looks colourful but is inspiring in its range of colour as well as texture.

PROJECT IDEA

Whether you're beginning with some newly purchased threads or a menagerie of hand-me-downs, begin a 'library' by storing them in simple plastic containers with clear plastic lids. Group them by colour as well as texture. The containers will build into a collection of knitting wool, tapestry wool, boucle, stranded cotton, cotton perle, suede strips, raffia, bubbly, crochet cotton in addition to pill bottles full of sparkling beads and sequins in co-ordinating colours.

The creative embroiderer is an enterprising individual when it comes to finding embroidery accessories and storage holders. Your family, friends and fellow embroiderers all have helpful ideas and suggestions.

Material

There are two types of canvas material for sale at most craft shops and department store counters. One is called double or Penelope canvas, which I don't recommend for creative canvas embroidery as the double woven threads limit the creative use of stitches.

Mono canvas, my recommendation, is a stiff woven fabric. It comes in three sizes suitable for embroidery — either ten, twelve or fourteen threads to the inch (2.5 cm). Ten-to-the-inch canvas has the largest holes, twelve-and fourteen-to-the-inch canvas having proportionately smaller holes than ten. Mono canvas is also available in sixteen, eighteen, twenty and twenty-two threads to the inch, but I prefer to work with the twelve- or fourteen-thread varieties. I find with these I can use the greatest variety of threads for the best effect.

Mono canvas may be used successfully for small projects. It is necessary to overlock (or secure) the edges of the seam allowance around the embroidery. Leave a seam allowance of ½ in. (12 mm) using a sewing machine, and around the edge zigzag two or three overlapping rows of machine stitchery around the edge. Alternatively, the edge can be sealed by running a line of white or clear adhesive along the edge of the seam allowance. However, this may give a stiffness to the edge which you don't prefer. I suggest that you consider the alternatives when the article is finished. You can make a decision at that time according to the materials you have on hand, the effect you desire, and your time limitations.

Overlocked canvas is a mono canvas with the intersecting threads sewn in place with cotton thread. My experience of overlocked canvas is that stitches which form eyelet holes cannot be pulled tightly enough to form a satisfactory eyelet hole. These 'unsuitable' stitches include all the eyelet variations such as the ray or fan stitch and the half circles. Furthermore, if the canvas is pulled firmly the overlocking threads tend to break. The overlocking thread also tends to hold the canvas in place around the broken thread preventing control of the shape of the hole. It is for these reasons that I avoid overlocked canvas for creative embroidery.

However, overlocked canvas is ideal for small projects

which will be made up into practical items, particularly in conjunction with the binding stitch (refer to Chapter 7 on Mounting and Making Up). Such small items include scissors cases, coin purses, wallets and belts.

Equipment

NEEDLES

Use blunt pointed, large-eyed needles called **tapestry needles** which come in various sizes. Buy a packet of tapestry needles in assorted sizes then work with a needle in accordance with your need. Choose the size which has an eye large enough to hold the required thread but not so big as to distort the holes of the canvas.

SCISSORS

1. A small pair of sharp embroidery scissors to cut and trim threads and yarns. Scissors can be inexpensive and basic or more expensive and decorative.

2. A large, old pair of fabric scissors to cut the canvas. I wouldn't suggest using your good fabric scissors as the canvas tends to loosen the holding screw thereby rendering the scissors unusable for finer fabrics. An old pair of fabric scissors can also be used for cutting paper and light cardboard.

FRAMES

I recommend a rectangular tapestry frame be used for all canvas embroidery. I never work canvas in the hand as it is my experience that the fabric becomes distorted from lack of tension control. Moisture from the hands also tends to soften and distort the canvas, particularly in warmer climates. There is a fair amount of size, or glue, used to stiffen the canvas, which causes distortion after the application of moisture.

Needlepoint pictures that are worked in tent stitch, a flat stitch, can be larger than the frame and rolled from one roller to another as the canvas is covered with stitches. Creative canvas work, however, by its very nature is raised and textured; therefore rolling it tightly around a roller flattens and spoils the texture. For this reason the size of the finished embroidery work should fit within the frame.

A simple and inexpensive frame without the rollers can be assembled as follows:

1. Buy a length of wooden beading used by builders for finishing off interior household joinery. This can be bought at a builders' hardware store and should measure about 1 in. to 1¼ in. (2.5 to 3 cm) wide.

2. Cut the beading into four required lengths allowing an extra 1½ in. to 2 in. (4 to 5 cm) at each end of each length.

3. Buy four screws approximately ¼ in. (6 mm) in diameter, with four matching butterfly wing nuts to fit the screws.

4. Drill a hole large enough to take these screws at each end of the four wooden lengths, at the required size.

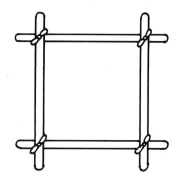

5. Overlap the four lengths as shown, inserting the screws and attaching and tightening the butterfly wing nuts to the screws.

6. To mount the canvas to this frame, a better tension is obtained by lacing the canvas to the four sides of the frame with lightweight string or unbreakable bri-nylon knitting yarn. From time to time, as required, this lacing can be tightened to maintain a firm tension.

Although it is not generally recommended that canvas work be done in a hoop, occasionally a small item could be done this way. But it is important that in such circumstances, the embroiderer takes care to stab stitch and not treat the canvas as hand-held fabric (where you take the needle through the fabric more than

---

On facing page, samples of canvas material available in white, ecru and some colours.

TOP ROW, left to right: 10 to 1 inch mono, 12 to 1 inch mono, 13 to 1 inch mono
2nd ROW, left to right: 14 to 1 inch mono, 16 to 1 inch mono, 18 to 1 inch mono
3rd ROW, left to right: 24 to 1 inch mono, 10 to 1 inch interlock, 12 to 1 inch interlock
4th ROW, left to right: 14 to 1 inch interlock, 10 to 1 inch Penelope striped waste canvas, 9 to 1 inch Penelope
BOTTOM ROW, left to right: 10 to 1 inch Penelope, 12 to 1 inch Penelope, No. 4 rug canvas

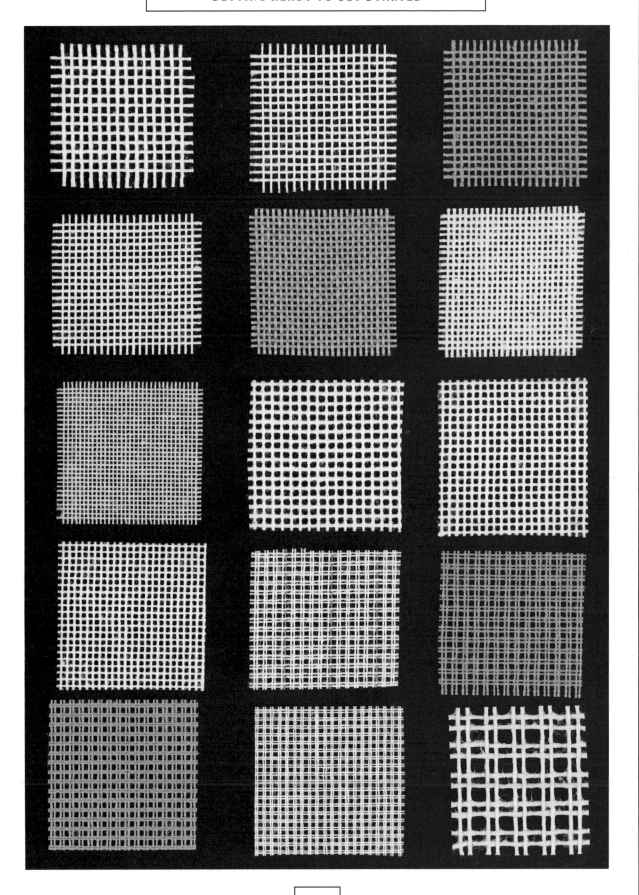

once before pulling the thread through). I recommend a wooden hoop with a screw adjustment be used. Follow these guidelines to set up the hoop:

1. Before using the hoop bind the inner ring of the hoop with bias binding, sewing the end in place with ordinary sewing thread. The bound inner ring prevents slipping of the fabric by holding it firmly in place.
2. Cut out a circle of canvas with a seam allowance of ¾ in. (2 cm) to 1 in. (2.5 cm) larger than the hoop. The hoop should not be larger than 8 in. (20 cm) in diameter.
3. Machine sew bias binding around the edge of the canvas. First, attach one side of the bias binding with machine zig-zag stitch. Then fold the bias binding along the centre and sew this down with another row of machine zigzag stitching on top of the first row of machine stitching, sandwiching the canvas in between the bias binding. (If bias binding is not sewn around the edge the canvas will scratch and irritate your hands as you work).
4. Place in hoop.

Illustrated in colour on page *i*.

THIMBLE
A thimble, once you have become accustomed to it, is invaluable for ease of work and preventing soreness and damage to your fingers. Decorative thimbles, like scissors, are gifts welcomed by other embroiderers, particularly if they are presented in an embroidered carry bag.

FURNITURE
Use a comfortable lounge chair with low arm rests, or sit at a table with the frame resting on the table. I find it helpful when sitting at a table to rest a book on the end of the frame to hold it in place. An occasional table nearby holds your threads, scissors, thimbles and other accessories.

LIGHTING
The most important piece of advice which I can give to you is always to use good light. Invest in an adjustable standard or table light that can be directed toward your embroidery. Overhead lights and lampshades are simply not adequate.

Preparing the Canvas
When cutting a piece of canvas for mounting on a frame treat the canvas as if it were a piece of fabric with grain. Always mount the canvas with the selvedge running vertically. To secure and reinforce the edges of the canvas, you can use one of two methods. First you can machine sew the edges of the canvas with two or three rows of zigzag or serpentine stitch. Alternatively, machine sew with either straight stitch, zigzag or serpentine stitch a length of bias binding or cotton tape to the front and on top of the edge of the canvas.

Attach two sides of the canvas to the two roller ends of the frame as follows:

1. Measure the roller ends of the frame with a ruler and make a permanent mark on the rollers' binding tape at the half-way points.

2. Mark the half-way point of the two sides of the canvas that are to be sewn to the frame's binding tape.
3. Match the two half-way points, canvas and roller tape, and pin canvas to tape as if they were two seams to be joined with a $\frac{1}{10}$ in. (3 mm) seam allowance.
4. With a double strand of sewing cotton oversew the two edges together.
5. Turn the rollers of the frame until the canvas is firm and taut, and secure the tension nuts.
6. Using fine string or strong bri-nylon thread, lace the remaining two sides of canvas to the other two ends of the frame. To ensure that the two sides of the canvas are straight lace both sides, loosely first before finishing off. Tighten the lacing of the two sides at the same time, ensuring straight even lines, then tie off with several buttonhole stitches. Leave a short tail of thread no more than 2 in. (5 cm) long.
7. The canvas should be firm and drum-taut. From time to time as you are working, the tension of the canvas will slip and this should be corrected by turning the rollers when necessary and tightening the tension screws.

Marking the Design
1. Outline the design lines on paper with black texta or a fine marking pen.
2. Pin the design in place to the back of the canvas.
3. Using a good light, mark the design on the canvas with a waterproof marking pen. *Note:* Care must be taken when white or pale threads are to be

used as dark markings might show through between the stitches. In this instance use a pale-coloured marking pen or sew in thread design lines that can be later removed if necessary.

Always mark the outside edge of the work as this keeps the eye within the space to be worked. If this line is not drawn in the eye takes in the size and shape of the frame and the proportions and scale of the work are affected.

Sometimes a B or 2B pencil can be used to mark the design onto canvas; however care needs to be taken to avoid the lead smudging. Be careful to draw fine, light lines of pencil, dusting lightly and blowing loose lead away.

If you are unable to see the design properly through the canvas, place the frame against a window to reveal clearly the design lines. You may also place the frame on a glass table top with a lamp shining up from underneath. Another method of transferring the design is to cut up a tracing or photostat copy of the major outlines, pin them onto the canvas and draw around the outline of the cut pieces.

PROJECT IDEA

I've found that embroiderers enjoy giving each other a gift of scissors decorated with an embroidered tab and/or tassels, or in a specially embroidered case.

2

TAKING THE FIRST STITCH

There are many stitches suitable to creative canvas embroidery; many of them are detailed in this chapter. You'll find that each stitch has endless possibilities, depending on your choice of colour and thread and which stitch and colour you choose to work next to it. This is where your individual style will differentiate your work from that of anyone else.

To follow the graphs of how to work the stitches it will help if you count the number of threads of the canvas fabric (graph lines), *not* the holes. Many canvas work stitches are based on the square; to begin with, it is advisable to start with this group. For example, cushion stitch can be worked covering a two-thread square, a four-thread square or a larger square. When you see the stitch as a square over, say, two threads it will make the understanding and working of all square stitches simpler. *A further hint*: I find it helpful and easier on the eyes to actually draw lightly in pencil on the threads of the canvas the square shape to be worked before beginning to work the stitch.

Methods of Working

The methods I suggest here are the results of my experience and efforts to obtain a sharp, clear, crisp edge to each stitch. You may agree with my sequence, or you may disagree and devise a method that suits you better. Whichever method you find best should produce sharp, clear edges forming holes or perforations between stitch units.

I refer to the stitches as the primary pattern, while I call the patterns created by the holes and perforations of distinct stitch-edges the secondary pattern. This secondary pattern can be an important feature of your design. Over time you will develop an awareness of this secondary pattern of holes or perforations, which can be very helpful when choosing stitches to interpret effects.

To give an example, small diagonal stitch and large diagonal stitch form a very distinctive secondary pattern of diagonal lines. Eyelet stitch is worked on a square and the secondary pattern created by the roundness of the centre hole can dominate the overall square shape. On the other hand, when eyelet stitch is worked in a half-dropped or irregular pattern, it takes on a different character as the secondary pattern changes to create different effects.

Covering the Canvas

The choice of thread for a particular stitch will determine how well the canvas is either covered or allowed to show through. This is a matter of individual taste. Remember that diagonal stitches, such as the mosaic and cushion stitches, cover the canvas much more than vertical or horizontal stitches such as Gobelin, Florentine, Hungarian, Parisian and others. When selecting a stitch consider the thickness of the thread that will cover the canvas adequately for your need. Alternatively you can choose a thread first then select a stitch which will best suit the chosen thread.

How to Start and Finish Off

When commencing on blank canvas tie a knot in the thread and put the needle down through the top of the canvas 2 in. (5 cm) away from where you wish to start, within the working area but not around the outside edge of the working area. As the stitchery covers the thread at the back it holds the thread in place. When you have worked up to where the knot is, the knot should be snipped off.

When you wish to start a new thread adjacent to an area which you've already worked, tie a knot at the end of the thread in your needle and attach it with two back or anchoring stitches to the back of a nearby worked area. Snip off the knot. This is called a waste knot. The reason the knot is needed is because the thread will usually pull through before the anchoring back stitches are in place. Proceed to the area to be worked.

I am often asked how far the wool should be allowed to travel from one place to another on the back of the work. I consider 1 in. to 2 in. (2.5 cm to 5 cm) a fairly tidy jump; if you are fastidious the thread can be run through the back of the stitched work to conceal a jump.

If you are working a particular thread and don't wish to use it all at once never leave it hanging freely at the back of the work. It will get in your path each time you work a stitch, and get caught up in loops. When your use for a particular thread is finished work a couple of anchoring stitches in the back of the work and snip off the rest. The remaining thread can be slipped through the canvas outside the working area at the front of the work until you need to use it again.

The most difficult stitch is always the *first* one, whichever that is! This applies to every new project, or even to every time you pick up your canvas or fabric. If you find that you can't think of how to start, just do any stitch — even if you have to take it out later or cover it with special effects.

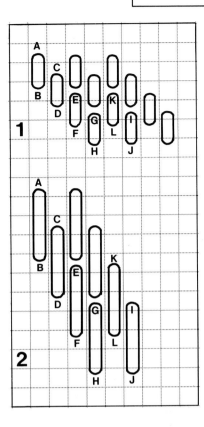

BRICK STITCH

This stitch is best worked vertically but can also be worked horizontally. It is a non-directional filling stitch effective for backgrounds and shaded areas. It can be worked over two threads (Figure 1) or four threads (Figure 2). Being a vertical stitch it requires a thicker thread to cover the canvas. Brick stitch over two threads is very useful for filling small areas, while it is a quick way of filling in large areas when worked over four threads.

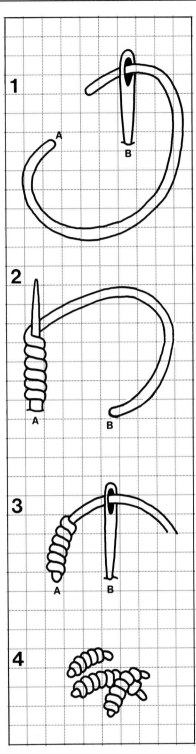

BULLION KNOT

1. To work bullion stitch in a frame, bring the needle out of the canvas at A, insert down at B. In the meantime hold the thread between A and B with your left hand. (Left handers please reverse.)

2. Place right hand under canvas and push needle out of canvas at A until at least three-quarters of the needle protrudes. Keep hold of the needle with the right hand under the canvas.

Wind the thread around the needle five to eight times (or as desired) with the left hand, using the right hand to turn the needle around to assist the winding. It is best to wind the thread around the thicker part of the needle, not too tightly and not too loosely. If the thread is wound too tightly it will be very difficult to pull the needle through; if the thread is too loose the bullion stitch could be uneven and untidy.

3. With the left hand, hold wound thread and needle firmly and with the right hand pull the needle gently through the coils. Tease the coils with the needle while firming the coiled stitch by pulling the thread. Insert needle down into B again and proceed to next stitch.

Uses
• Bullion knots can be worked side by side, symmetrically or asymmetrically, or diagonally on top of each other
• If a looped stitch effect is required, take a short distance between A and B
• If a flat effect is desired take a distance between A and B that will allow the stitch to lay straight, depending on the thickness of your thread and the number of times it is wound around the needle.

◄

7/407153

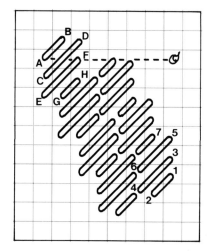

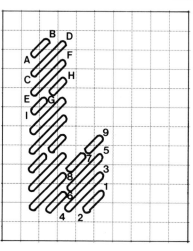

CRISS CROSS ▼

Commencing with a knot approximately 2¼ in. (6 cm) away (refer to earlier in this chapter on how to start and finish off), come out at 1. Take the needle down into A, come out at 2 and take the needle down into B, continuing in this manner until the nine straight stitches have been worked. In order to obtain an even geometrical effect the diagram needs to be carefully followed.

CASHMERE

This stitch is worked diagonally. Come out of the canvas at A, down into B, out at C, down into D, out at E and down into F, out at G and down into H. The last stitch G–H is at the same time the last of the rectangular diagonal stitch and the first of the next rectangular unit which is the basis of this stitch. The adjacent rows are worked in the same manner but interlock. This stitch resembles small diagonal stitch but is based on a rectangle whereas small diagonal stitch is based on a square.

CASHMERE VARIATION

This is a variation of cashmere stitch that resembles cushion stitch but is worked as a rectangle instead of a square. The stitch is worked vertically from top to bottom or from bottom up, but preferably in the order illustrated to obtain best result for a crisp edge of even perforations.

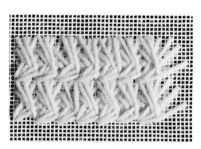

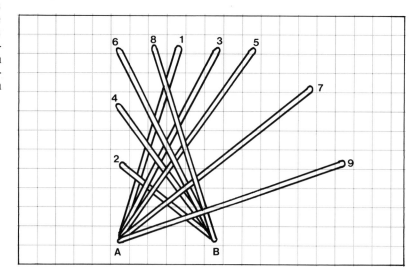

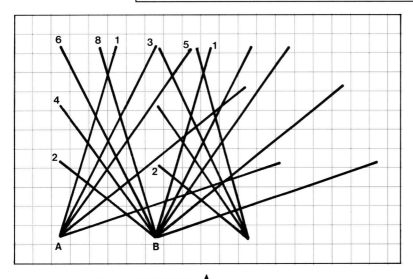

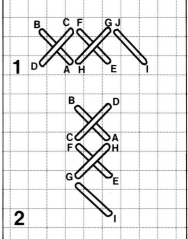

CRISS CROSS VARIATION ▲

Should a free, airy effect be required this stitch is ideal. Work the nine straight stitches in the order shown, but instead of meticulously counting the threads between each stitch work the stitches in a radiating arc. Repeat each unit in this manner and then work succeeding rows either partly on top of the previous row or work two rows back to back. This variation is very useful for interpreting feathers, palm leaves and light lacy effects which can be varied *ad infinitum* by changing threads. Where spaces are left between the stitches, you can choose to leave canvas showing, or work tent stitch.

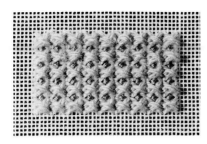

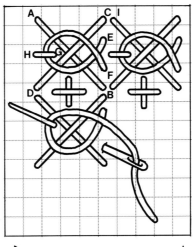

▶ CROSS, CHAINED ▲

Each chained cross is completed before proceeding to the next one. Come out at A, down at B, out at C, down at D, then out at E to commence the chain. Form a loop with the thread. Holding the loop with the left thumb take needle down at F coming out at G. Pull the thread gently with an even tension at G so that the chain stitch is made firm, not too tight and not too loose. Take needle down into H and then out at I to start the next stitch. If you wish to cover the space left between the rows, work an upright cross.

CROSS, DIAGONAL

This stitch, worked as in Figure 1 for an even result, can be worked over two threads square (Figure 1), one thread square (Figure 3), or more threads. Care needs to be taken to choose an appropriate thickness of thread which will cover the canvas adequately but not so thickly that the stitch won't be recognised. For the best result, ensure that the second stitches forming the crosses are all worked in the same direction. This will become second nature once the rhythm of the stitch is mastered. This stitch can be worked horizontally as in Figure 1, vertically as in Figure 2, or from right to left as in Figure 3.

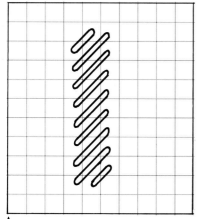

▲CROSS, DIAGONAL HALF OR SATIN

This is a very useful stitch, particularly as a space filler in random texture. Work the diagonal half cross over two threads square, starting and finishing with a tent stitch.

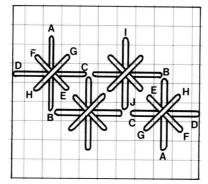

▲ CROSS, DIAMOND

First work an upright cross over four threads. Then cover it with a diagonal cross over two threads, creating a diamond shape. This stitch can also be worked horizontally from right to left, as shown in the second row of the diagram.

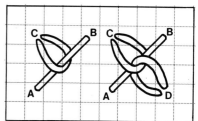

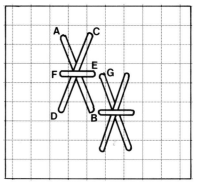

CROSS, HOUND'S TOOTH▲

Bring thread out at A, down at B to form a half cross over five threads square, out at C, loop thread over and under A-B and down into C, out at D and under and around A-B and through the previous loop and down into D again. This is an attractive textured stitch which can be worked over any number of squares, provided the thread used is adequate to cover the canvas or conversely, not so thick so that the effect is lost. This stitch is most effective worked in two colours: one colour for the half cross A-B and another for the two interlaced loops.

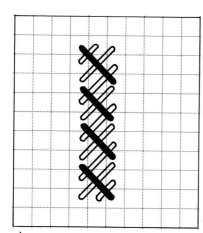

▲ CROSS, SATIN VARIATION

After working an area of diagonal half cross select a contrasting thread in a lighter weight and colour and whip the diagonal cross in the opposite direction every two threads. Further variations to this stitch may be obtained by working the diagonal cross over more than two threads, and whipping in an irregular manner instead of evenly over every two threads.

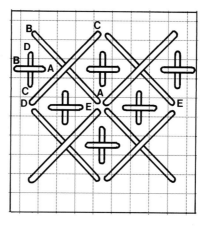

▲ CROSS, DOUBLE

First, work diagonal cross stitches over four threads. Then come back to fill the spaces formed by the crosses with a vertical or upright cross. This is a very attractive filling stitch when worked in contrasting or harmonious colours.

▲CROSS, INTERLOCKING AND TIED

Worked the same as oblong interlocking cross with the addition of a bar across the intersection of the cross, which adds more texture to this stitch.

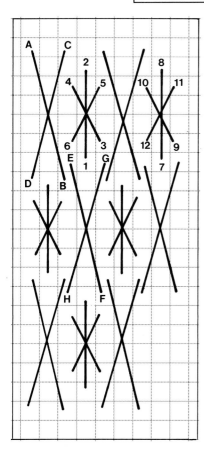

CROSS, LARGE DOUBLE FILLER

Long vertical crosses are first worked over two vertical by-seven horizontal threads in a diagonal manner so that each cross overlaps the other by one thread of canvas. After the long crosses have been worked, fill the space with the elongated cross in a matching or contrasting colour.

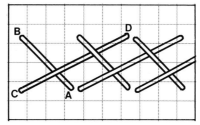

CROSS, LONG LEGGED

This stitch may at first seem difficult to do but is actually a repeat of the same cross, A-B-C-D over and over again. Care should be taken when counting the threads on the top and bottom lines. This stitch has an attractive texture which resembles corduroy velvet when used as a large space filler or background, but doesn't look so effective in a small area.

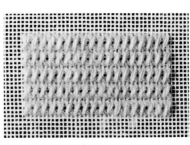

CROSS, OBLONG

Worked in the same manner as diagonal cross over two and four threads. Work the first row from left to right and the second row from right to left. Work an anchoring stitch between rows at the back of the canvas.

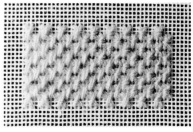

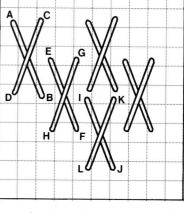

CROSS, OBLONG INTERLOCKING

Although worked differently, this stitch is similar to oblong cross, but interlocking or half-dropped and more successful worked in a diagonal manner. It must be worked over an even number of horizontal threads so that the half-dropped effect will work out.

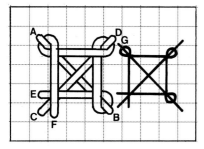

CROSS, PLAITED

Each stitch unit is completed before proceeding to the next one. Come out at A, down at B, out at C, down at D then out at E. The plaiting is worked around each arm of the cross without going into the canvas until the last plait, when the needle is taken down at F. Commence next plaited cross by coming out at G and repeating the above.

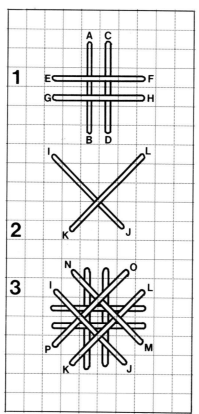

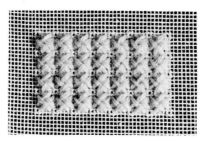

CROSS, PLAITED AND INTERLACED

First, work the double upright cross over five threads square, then the herringbone cross I-J-K-L and lastly M-N-O-P, with O-P threaded under I-J to give the proper interlaced finish. This is a very attractive stitch which can be worked symmetrically or asymmetrically but not half dropped, as there are an uneven number of threads). This stitch is also attractive combined in random texture. It can be worked without the double upright cross, although in this case canvas will show through.

Small areas of canvas show at the corners of this stitch and these can be filled with small eyelets over two threads square in a finer thread for a very attractive effect. A small upright cross is also suitable for these spaces.

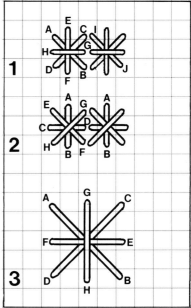

CROSS, SMYRNA

This is a very attractive and useful stitch. The diagonal cross can be worked first over two threads square (Figure 1), or the upright cross first. Figure 2 shows the diagonal cross worked last and Figure 3 shows Smyrna over four threads square. It should be noted that when the upright cross is worked last there is a choice of whether to work the horizontal or the vertical bar of the upright cross last, as a quite different effect can be obtained from either.

Figure 1 shows the horizontal bar worked last while Figure 3 shows the vertical bar worked last.

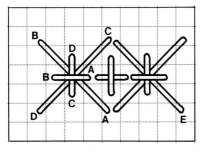

CROSS, SMYRNA VARIATION

Work a diagonal cross over four threads square, covering it with a vertical cross over two threads. With the same or contrasting thread work a small upright cross over two threads square in the remaining space.

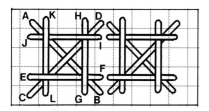

CROSS, SQUARED AND INTERLACED

Work a diagonal cross A,B,C,D over four threads square then come out at E, go down into the canvas at F, out at G, down at H, out at I, down at J, out at K and before going down into L take the needle and thread under E-F to complete the interlaced pattern. This stitch is very attractive in two colours and covers the canvas well.

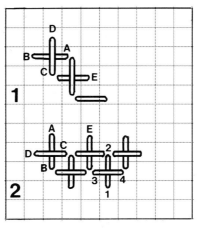

CROSS, VERTICAL OR UPRIGHT

This stitch may be worked diagonally or horizontally over two threads and can be crossed either vertically or horizontally. It can also be worked from right to left, as shown in Figure 2.

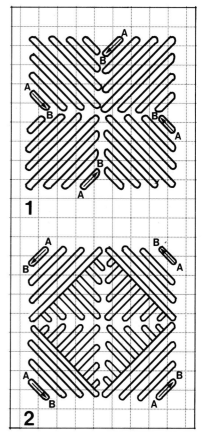

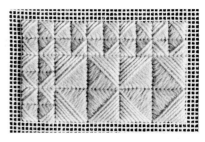

CUSHION, CROSSED

First work four cushions (see large cushion stitch). Then, in a contrasting or matching thread, preferably of a lighter weight and thickness to the thread used to work the cushion, work half a cushion stitch over the first but in the opposite direction. Six strands of stranded cotton, coton perle or other thread of suitable thickness work well on this stitch. For a neat, crisp edge work the cushions and the crossed cushions as in Figure 1, commencing each cushion as A-B and following the direction of the arrows.

Pre-planning (the direction

of) the first cushion stitches can create beautiful effects, with light reflecting on the different directions of the crossed cushions.

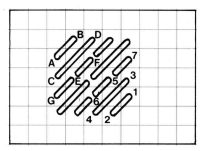

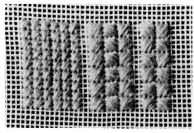

Large cushion and mosaic cushion stitch

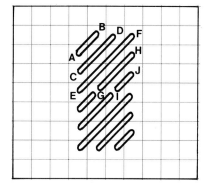

CUSHION, LARGE

Work this stitch in the same manner as small cushion except for an extra stitch. Large cushion is worked over three threads square and can also be worked over four or more threads square.

CUSHION, MOSAIC OR SMALL

Bring needle out at A, approaching from the opposite direction in order to create a crisp perforation at A. For best effect work this stitch vertically from bottom to top. Before starting another row always take a small anchoring stitch in the back of the last stitch. Cushion stitches worked over a square of two canvas threads can be used as a filler, a line stitch or on their own.

Cushion stitches illustrated in colour on page v.

DIAGONAL ▶

Both Figures 1 and 2 are worked diagonally and can be stitched from top to bottom or bottom to top. However, to obtain the best result, follow the order of working as set out in the diagrams and work the diagonal rows from right to left. Diagonal stitch forms a quite different texture when a row of tent stitch is worked between each diagonal row.

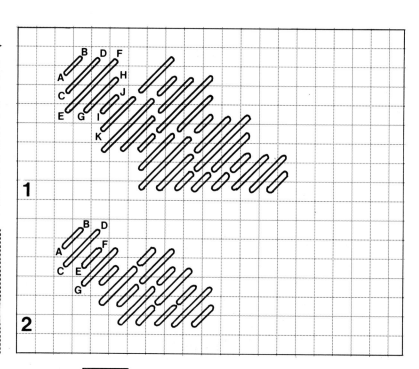

DIAMOND PATTERNED FILLINGS

These diamond patterns make very attractive textured fillers as the diamond-shaped perforations create a lovely secondary pattern. The different patterns shown in these diagrams all have this secondary pattern, but the texture is different in each one. Try different textures of diamonds together to experiment. For the variation as shown in Figure 3, come out at A and down into B, out at C and down into B again, out at D,E,F,G,H respectively and down into B each time. An eyelet hole forms at B.

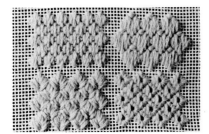

DIAMOND LEAF ►

This stitch is just as much at home in this group of diamond fillers as it is when used as an isolated leaf stitch. Like leaf stitch, it is easier to work from the bottom to the top in order to facilitate the overlap of each row.

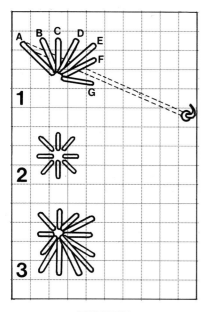

EYELET

Eyelet stitch is a beautiful, versatile, stitch that has many effects and applications — either on its own or combined with other stitches. To create a well-made, crisp-edged eyelet the following instructions should be helpful:

1. Start the eyelet at A coming from the opposite direction, not from above as the perforation at the edge of the stitch will be covered, creating an uneven and untidy effect.

2. Stretch the hole in the centre by pushing the canvas threads back with the needle or stiletto.

3. Pull the first few stitches very firmly making a large hole in the middle, allowing the rest of the stitches to fit through the hole and leaving a crisp, even eyelet.

4. Always insert the needle down into the centre eyelet hole, not up the hole from the back of the canvas as this will cause the edges to be tightened towards the centre, not the centre pulled out to the edge.

5. When the eyelet has been worked turn the frame over and anchor the thread with one stitch in the back of the eyelet stitch — directly behind the last stitch, without covering the eyelet hole.

6. Proceed to the next eyelet stitch without taking the thread across the back of the eyelet hole, even if this means making another anchoring stitch in the back of the work.

7. If the eyelet hole is closed from a buildup of threads the cause could be that the thread is too thick; therefore change to a finer thread, *or*, the tension has not been tight enough from the *first* stitch.

8. Eyelet stitches may be worked in any direction as long as the anchoring stitch is made at the back and the thread does not cover the eyelet hole.

To make a symmetrical eyelet stitch with a centre hole an even number of threads must be covered. Figure 1 is over four threads, Figure 2 is worked over two threads and so forth. If the eyelet hole does not need to be centred then any number of threads may be covered. Refer to Figure 3. Attractive effects are made by grouping symmetrical and asymmetrical eyelet stitches together with or without random filling stitches (refer to random filling stitches). When working asymmetrical eyelets it may be necessary to miss a stitch when a buildup of threads occurs.

Always finish a thread off and don't leave threads hanging at the back of the work as they become tangled and messy and interfere with proper working.

Note: This stitch cannot be effectively worked on overlocked or oversewn canvas. The canvas and oversewn thread do not give way unless one of the threads snaps, and this usually results in an uneven, irregular hole.

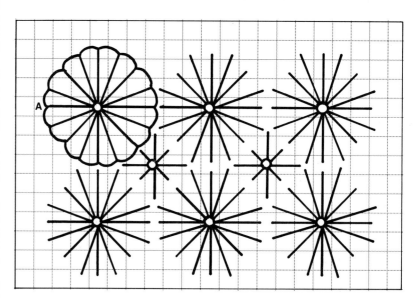

▲ EYELET CIRCLES — BUTTONHOLED ▶

Work the buttonholed eyelets first. (For directions on the buttonhole stitch see Chapter 5.) Then, with a contrasting or matching thread, fill the spaces in between with straight eyelets, as shown in the diagram. The diagram shows one buttonholed eyelet; the rest are shown as straight eyelets to show more clearly the holes to be worked.

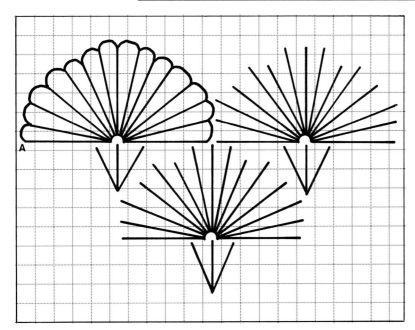

EYELET HALF-CIRCLES ◀ — BUTTONHOLED

Worked in the same manner as half eyelet or fantail, using buttonhole stitch instead of straight stitch. (Again, see Chapter 5 for the buttonhole stitch.) As the buttonhole stitch will cover the edge of the eyelet, only three filling stitches are required instead of five. Two or three rows of this stitch edged with tent stitch make a very attractive border.

For ease of working, start from the top row working down and from left to right.

▲

EYELET, DIAMOND ▶

Work the eyelet in the same manner as the eyelet stitch but in a diamond shape, making an anchoring stitch in the back of each stitch before proceeding to the next diamond. This stitch creates spaces between each unit that can be filled with back stitches in a coton perle, six stranded cotton or other suitable matching or contrasting thread.

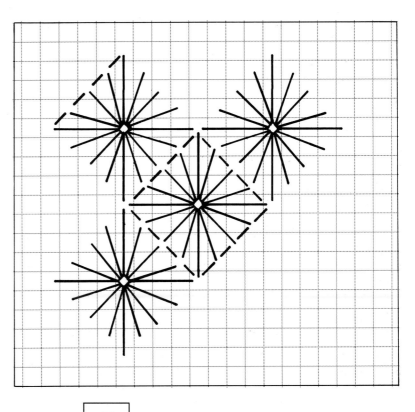

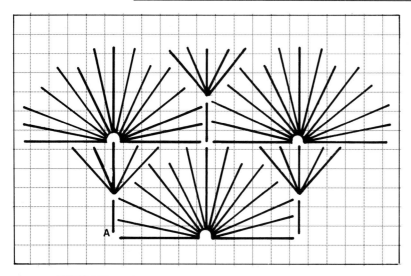

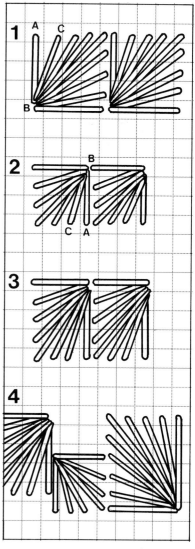

▲ EYELET, HALF OR FANTAIL ▶

Work the half eyelet, take an anchoring stitch in back of the eyelet stitch. Then work the next half eyelet, again taking an anchoring stitch before proceeding to the next half eyelet. Complete all the half eyelets and in a matching or contrasting thread work the straight stitches to fill the gaps. Work from the bottom row upwards and from right to left.

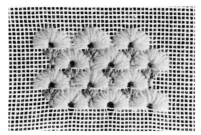

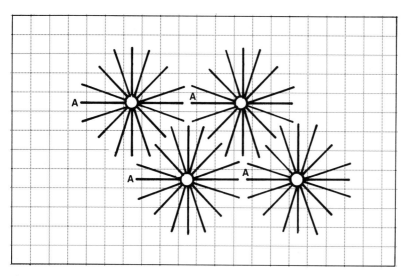

▲ EYELET, ROUND

Refer to general instructions for eyelet stitch when working this stitch in horizontal rows. Round eyelets are easiest worked in rows from right to left, commencing each eyelet at A and taking an anchoring stitch at the back of each round eyelet unit. A finer thread is preferable to avoid buildup in the eyelet hole.

FAN OR RAY

This is a very attractive stitch that is best worked in a reasonably thin thread in relation to the canvas size as the stitches pile on top of each other and can clog up the eyelet hole. As in eyelet stitch go down into the hole at B, first having enlarged the hole with a needle or stiletto. The stitch is worked as a square with the eyelet hole either at the top, bottom, or left or right of the stitch, as in Figures 1, 2 and 3. It may also be worked in an irregular manner as a rectangle and/or with the eyelet holes pointing in various directions.

When necessary, work a back or anchoring stitch

behind each ray stitch unit to ensure that the edges have an even, crisp finish of perforations.

For ease of working this stitch the following suggestions are made:

• When the eyelet hole B is at the bottom of the stitch, as in Figure 1, work the rows of ray stitches from the bottom upwards.

• When the eyelet hole B is at the top of the stitch, as in Figure 2, work the rows from the top down.

• When the eyelet holes are at random, as in Figure 4, the canvas may show between some of the units. This can be covered by back stitches in a contrasting or matching finer thread.

• When working large scale ray stitches a buildup of stitches may occur. To alleviate the buildup, skip a hole in the canvas and don't work every stitch. If the built-up effect is suitable to your requirement, work all the stitches or add more.

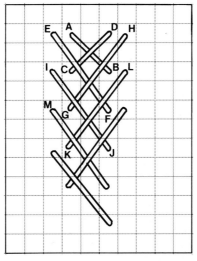

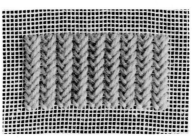

FERN

This is a beautiful textured stitch suitable as a filler, a line, or in small blocks for random texture. After the commencing stitches A-B and C-D are worked, the rest follow the same pattern: out at E, down four and across three threads to F, back across two threads to G and up four and across three threads to H.

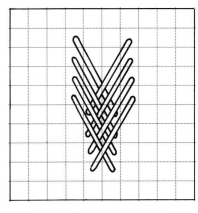

FERN, VARIATION

This stitch is worked similarly to fern but is over three threads at the top of the cross and only over one thread at the bottom of the cross. As in fern stitch it is four threads vertically. This also is an attractive filler, line or random texture and is very useful as a 'stem' for flowers.

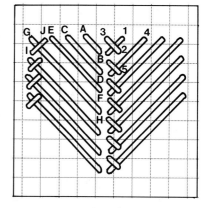

FISHBONE

This is a diagonal satin stitch over four threads square. Each stitch is crossed at one side with a tent stitch, and the rows form a chevron pattern. For the first vertical row work A-B, C-D, E-F and G-H. Come out at I and go down into J to form the tent stitch. Repeat G-H and I-J for the rest of the row. In the second vertical row come out at I and down into B of the first row, out at 2 and down into 3. Out at 4, down into D, out at 5 and down into B. Follow the diagram in this manner to the bottom of the row.

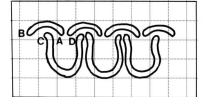

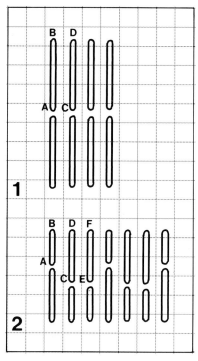

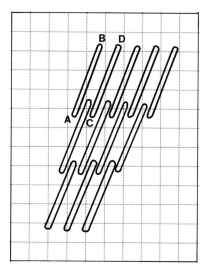

GHIORDES KNOT

Bring thread out at A, down into B and out at C. Form a loop with the thread, holding it in place with the thumb while taking the thread down into D. Come out at A again and repeat. As with velvet stitch, Ghiordes knot may be left in even or uneven loops to form a rich knubbly effect; or when the area is completely worked cut the loops with a very sharp pair of embroidery scissors and trim the pile to your requirements. Work this stitch in horizontal rows from the bottom row upwards. Commence each succeeding row two horizontal threads above the previous row.

Ghiordes knot is used by weavers. It differs from velvet stitch in that it is quicker to work. It may not be as secure as velvet stitch when the loops are cut to form a pile.

GOBELIN

This is another form of satin stitch worked in vertical lines over virtually any number of threads and in different patterns and groupings. This stitch can be worked from left to right and then right to left without difficulty, but also requires a thicker thread to cover the canvas well.

GOBELIN — ENCROACHING

This is a form of diagonal satin stitch worked in horizontal rows. Follow the diagram, coming out at A, up four horizontal threads, across one vertical thread and down into B. Each stitch after that is worked parallel to A-B. Each row encroaches or overlaps the previous one by one thread of the canvas. This is an attractive filler and background stitch. It can be shaded very successfully with different tones and colours.

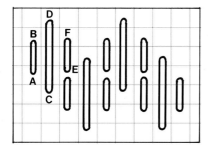

HUNGARIAN

A form of satin stitch similar to Parisian, worked vertically in groups of three over two threads, four threads and two threads of canvas; then miss a space and work another group of three. The next line is worked the same as the first, but it interlocks with the first as shown in the diagram. This stitch can be worked in alternate rows from left to right and right to left. Being vertical, it requires thicker thread to cover the canvas properly.

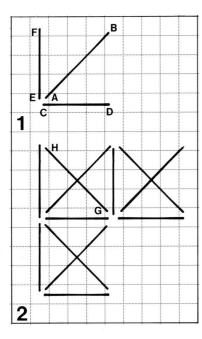

ITALIAN TWO SIDED

This stitch is worked over four threads square, as in the diagram. It makes an interesting and unique texture when worked over a reasonably sized area, but looks just as interesting on its own or included in a random texture.

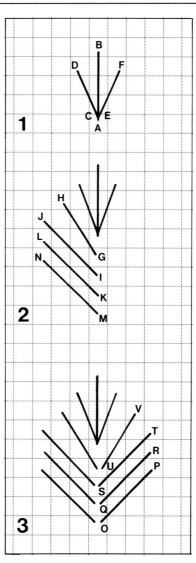

LEAF

First work the top three stitches as shown in the diagram, then work down the left side of the stitch and up the right side. To work the leaves in an interlocking manner, work the rows from the bottom up.

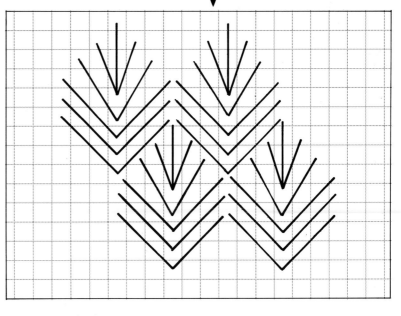

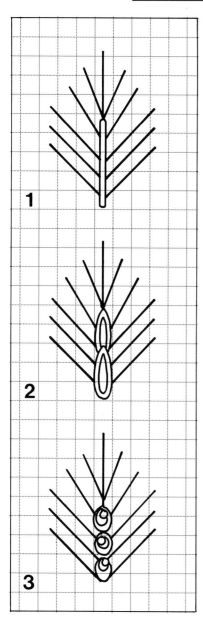

Leaf variations

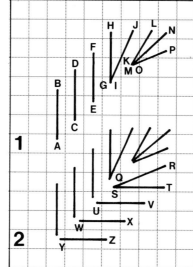

Diagonal leaf stitch

to right. As shown in the leaf stitch variations the leaves can be finished off with a stem of straight stitch, French knots, chain stitch or back stitches.

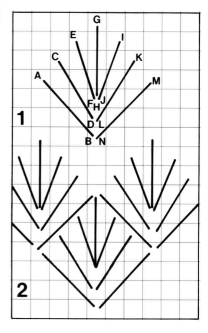

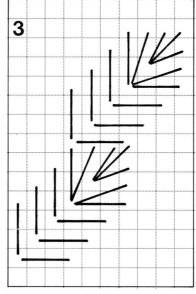

LEAF, VARIATIONS

These three variations show different ways of finishing off the leaves:

1. Using one long straight stitch (Figure 1)

2. Using chain stitches (Figure 2)

3. Using French knots (Figure 3)

4. Another alternative is three back stitches. Matching or contrasting threads and colours may be used.

LEAF, DIAGONAL

Care is required in carefully following the diagram to work the diagonal leaf. To interlock the leaves to make a filler, work the rows from the bottom up in diagonal rows from left

LEAF, DIAMOND

Work the leaf as in the diagram; as with all interlocking leaf stitch fillers work the rows from the bottom up.

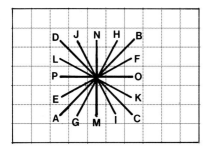

LEVIATHAN

Although this stitch appears to resemble Rhodes stitch, its texture is different. It is comprised of a number of cross stitches worked one on top of the other until the square is filled, forming a small mound in the centre.

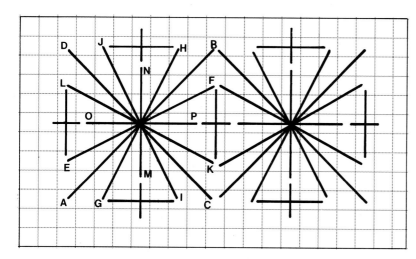

LEVIATHAN, VARIATION 1

Work a leviathan stitch with the cross formed by M-N-O-P having shorter arms than the others. Come back afterwards and fill in the spaces with cross stitches over four by two threads, as shown in the diagram.

LEVIATHAN, VARIATION 2

Figure 1 shows the leviathan stitch formed not by overlapping crosses, but by straight stitches down into the centre (as an *eyelet* stitch). The last vertical cross over four threads each way virtually covers the eyelet hole. Although at first the two variations appear to be the same, a very different effect is created. At the centre of the stitch in variation 1, the cross stitches form a small mound; variation 2 is quite flat in the centre.

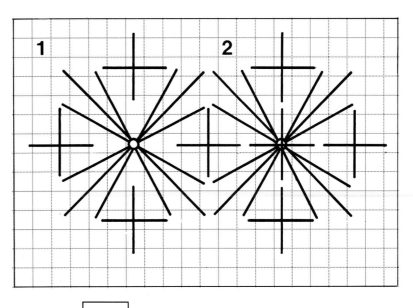

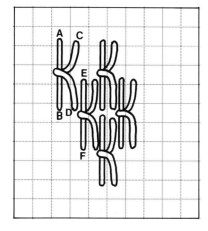

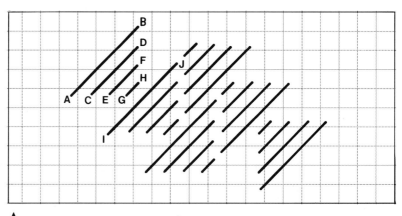

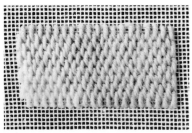

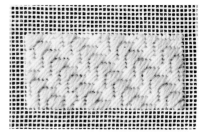

▲ MILANESE ►

Milanese stitch is comprised of diagonal rows of half cushions. The cushion in every second row points in the same direction and each row interlocks.

LINK SURFACE

This is a very attractive non-directional textured stitch. Non-directional means that the stitch creates an all-over knubbly texture without the perforations making a dominating secondary pattern. Come out at A, go down into B, come out at C, lace under A-B (not through the canvas) then down into D. This stitch is easiest worked in a diagonal manner from the top working down and from left to right. It is very effective when used for shading.

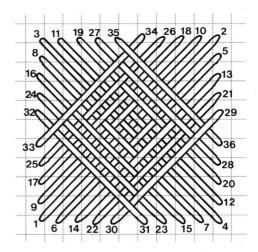

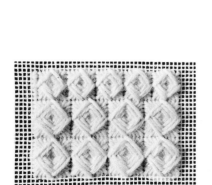

◄ NORWICH OR WAFFLE ▲

Norwich is a decorative feature stitch, the working of which requires careful attention to the instructions. The stitch must be worked over a square of uneven threads to obtain the result in the diagram. Work according to the diagram but note that the last stitch 35-36 is passed under stitch 29-30 to give the proper uniformity to the raised diamond effect that this stitch has. If the stitch is worked over an even number of threads, the effect will be slightly different: at the four points of the raised diamond the stitches will go into the same hole instead of overlapping. When learning this stitch ensure that you have enough thread to complete each unit.

OBLIQUE, HORIZONTAL

A very sloping diagonal satin stitch that requires a short filling stitch at the beginning and end of each row. ►

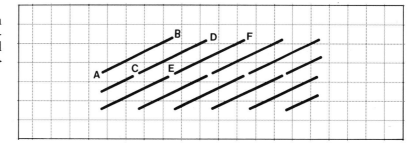

ORIENTAL

◄ ▼

This stitch creates a very interesting pattern of diagonal satin stitches that is seen at its best over a larger area.

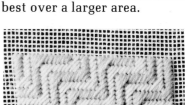

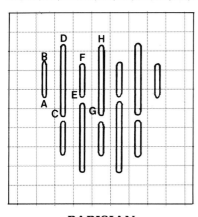

PETAL

◄

Commencing at A, work the straight stitches first as an eyelet. Then bring the needle out at B, a point under a group of straight stitches near the centre. Lace the thread several times under the straight stitches, spiralling out to the edge, then make four anchoring stitches as shown in the diagram. This stitch should be worked on an even number of threads.

▲

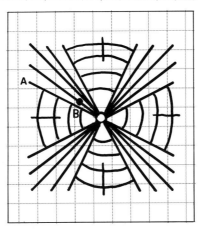

PARISIAN

This stitch is a form of satin stitch, worked alternately over two vertical threads of canvas and four threads of canvas, from left to right and then right to left. Remember that as this is a vertical stitch the thread required to cover the canvas best will need to be thicker than it would for a diagonal stitch.

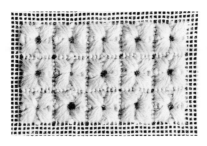

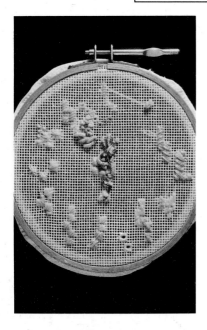

Two thread
- Tent
- Half cross (diagonal satin) — start and finish with a tent stitch, small eyelet, bullion and French knots, beads and diagonal cross
- Smyrna cross
- Whipped half cross

Two or more threads
Any of the above plus the following:
- Rhodes
- Fan or ray
- Crossed cushion
- Eyelet
- Wheatsheaf
- Roumanian
- Whipped half cross

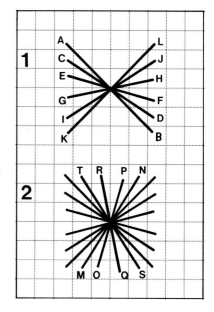

RANDOM FILLING STITCHES (RANDOM TEXTURE)

When creating a texture of different isolated stitches in a random manner, as in the sampler from Chapter 3, spaces of unworked canvas remain to be covered. Depending on the number of threads available to be worked I suggest the following stitches as space fillers:

One thread
- Tent and diagonal cross
- Bullion, French knots, cross, beading

RHODES

The basis of this stitch is satin stitch, worked in a spiral on a square grid. Although it uses a fair bit of thread, being as raised on the back as the front, it is a very beautiful textured stitch with numerous possibilities in creative canvas embroidery. Rhodes stitch can be worked over any number of even or uneven threads, preferably not less than three threads square (the effect is lost when it is worked on a very small scale). The stitch may be worked in rows of even blocks as a filler, in staggered uneven blocks for an uneven texture, or between two lines with the spaces filled using tent stitch. When finishing each Rhodes stitch, take the thread to the back of the work in the direction from which the last stitch came and make a small back or anchoring stitch into the underside of the Rhodes stitch.

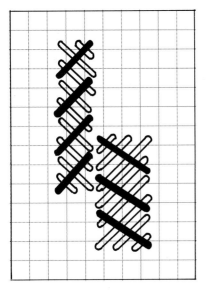

Whipped half cross

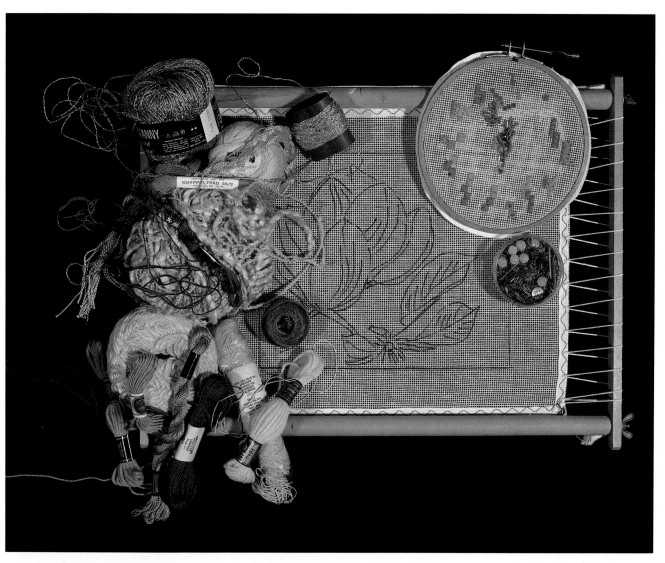

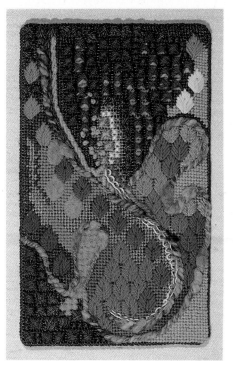

Above. Roller frame and hoop prepared for embroidery. Any type of thread may be considered. See page 14.

Far left. *Seaweed* (author)—couching, Rhodes, leaf, Pekinese, Smyrna cross, Portuguese knotted stem, basketweave, French knot, bullion. 36 x 26 cm (14 x 10 in).

Left. *Seashore* (author)—cross large double filler, Ghiordes knot, diamond eyelet and back stitch, oriental, diamond cross, detached buttonhole, buttonholed ring and washers. 36 x 26 cm (14 x 10 in).

I

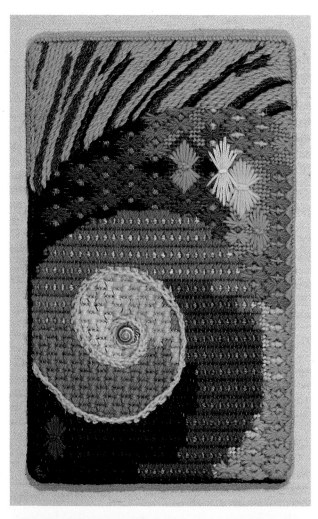

Left. *Shell* (author) — variations of wheatsheaf, stem, basketweave. 36 x 26 cm (14 x 10 in).

Below. *Sea and Shore* (author)—designs and colour inspired by shells and beach. Back row, left to right, notebook cover, hexagonal pincushion, box, cushion; front row, left to right, pencil holder, paper weight, bookmark, luggage tag, spectacle case, serviette ring. See Chapter 6.

Left. *South Beach* (author)—buttonhole, Smyrna cross, eyelet, basketweave, French knot, beads, needleweaving, detached buttonhole. The shell sits in a hole cut in the canvas and is surrounded by rows of detached buttonhole. 38 x 30 cm (15 x 12 in).

Below. *Hydrangeas* (author) —workbag, needlecase, pincushion and scissors tab. Mosaic, detached buttonhole, needleweaving, beads. Velvet rouleaux ties threaded through buttonholed rings held in place with canvas tabs finished with the binding stitch. 30 x 25 cm (12 x 10 in).

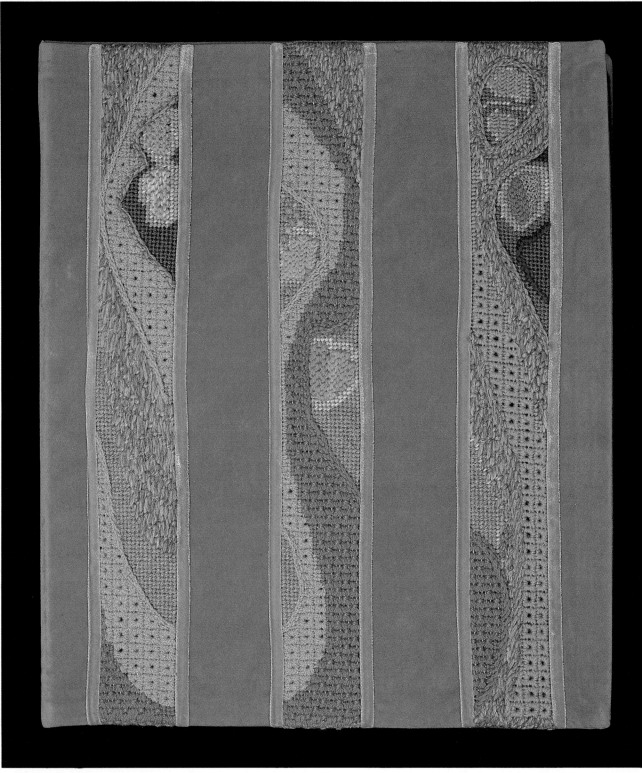

Pebbles (author)—book cover—Roumanian, square eyelet, wheatsheaf half dropped, padded raised stem band, basketweave, Smyrna cross. The three strips of canvas were applied to suede fabric and the raw edges concealed with hand stitched velvet ribbon. 40 x 34 cm (16 x 13 in).

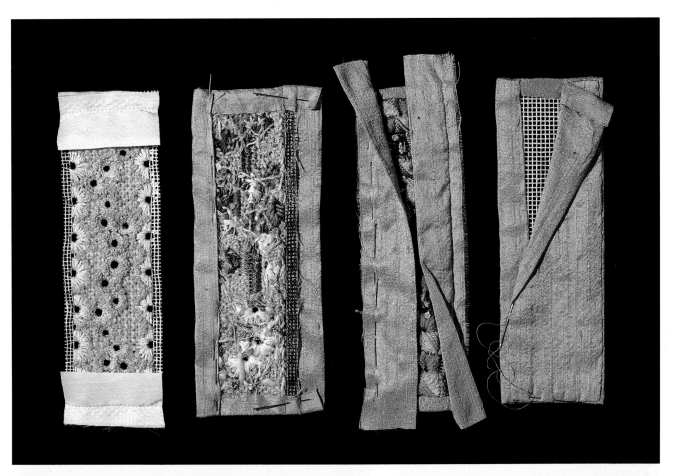

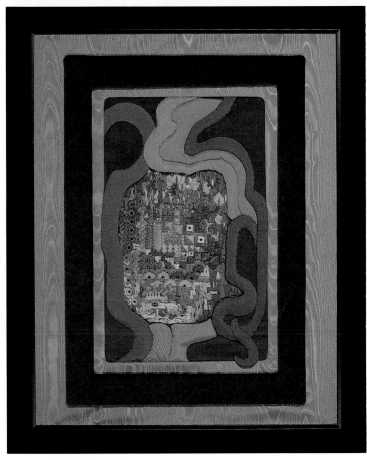

Top. *Bookmark* (author) — see page 90 for finishing-off instructions.

Left. *Art Nouveau* (author)—based on the First Project—see page 48.

Above. Detail *Art Nouveau* — note use of wheatsheaf stitch which has been worked in many sizes, crossed to one end as well as at the middle, units horizontally overlapping vertical units with varieties of thread. Cushion stitches have been decorated with straight stitches in shiny thread. 51 x 41 cm (20 x 16 in). See pages 27 and 28.

Left. *Three Cylinders* (Eileen Gale)—the two larger cylinders are based on the First and Second Projects and the third cylinder designed as a gift for a friend. See pages 48 and 49.

Below. *Effie's Inspirations* (June Fiford)—based on the First and Second Projects. Note effective use of unworked canvas. Panel 26 x 20 cm (10 x 8 in), cylinder 7½cm (3 in) diameter and height. See pages 48 and 49.

South Beach Triptych (author)—rainforest: applied leather, link surface.
Wheatsheaf half dropped, criss cross, detached buttonhole, Smyrna cross,
upright cross, basketweave, square eyelet, Rhodes, diagonal leaf,
needleweaving, raised close herringbone. The vines are starched, crocheted
wool and the leaves are held in place with a satin stitched wired edge.
Pelican: padded applique, detached buttonhole, brick, basketweave,
Smyrna cross, straight stitch, overlapping rows of criss cross. 62 x 58 cm
(25 x 23 in).

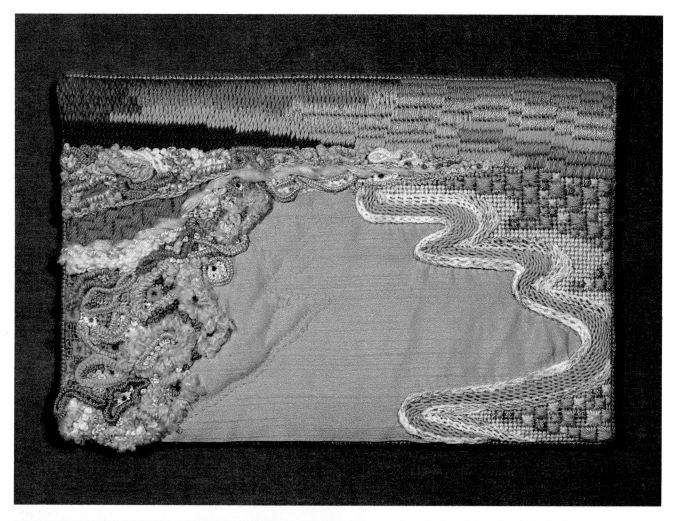

Above. *South Beach Triptych* (author)— beach:
gobelin and encroaching gobelin, oriental,
square eyelet, couching, twisted buttonhole
rings. Rhodes, raised stem band, heavy chain,
French knot. 40 x 30 cm (16 x 12 in).

Left. DETAIL *Beach*—note twisted buttonhole
rings—see page 90.

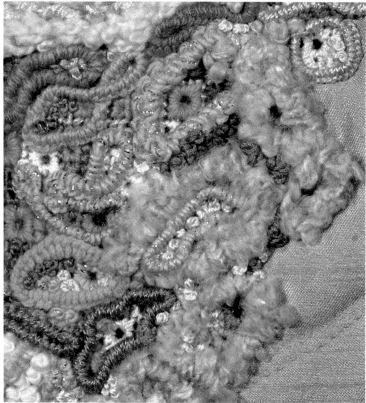

Bride's Reticule (left) (author)—round and half circle buttonholed eyelets, raised stem band, woven webs, re-embroidered buttonhole stitch, beads, French knots, twisted cord. 8½ x 10 cm (3½ x 4 in).

Jewel Box (right) (author)—three layers criss cross, square eyelets, padded areas of raised stem band, needleweaving, French knots, beads, detached buttonhole, twisted cord, embroidered and needlewoven tassels. 8½ x 20 cm (3½ x 8 in).

Top. *Jewel box* (author)—couched boucle, woven webs, ray, Rhodes, buttonholed and re-embroidered eyelets, beads, French knots. See page 64 for couching. 12 x 9 cm (5 x 3 in).

Left. *Bernie's Wave* (Susan Walter)—brick stitch, French knots, beads, cushion, rice, Rhodes, basketweave. 46 x 33 cm (18 x 13 in).

Above. DETAIL—top left hand quarter.

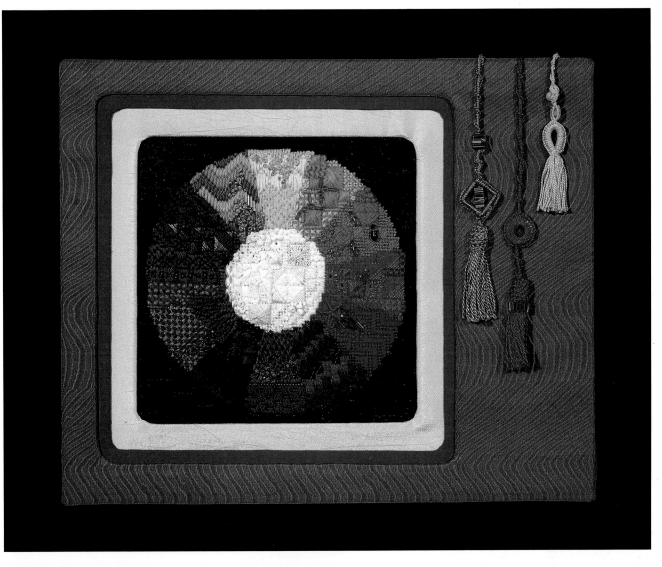

Above. *Twelve Part Colour Circle* (Susan Walter)—a study of colour, stitches, tassels and recessed mounting. See pages 52 and 53. 31 x 38 cm (12 x 15 in).

Left. DETAIL—centre.

Botany Bay Bark (author)—a beautiful knot of bark was tied and glued to the canvas. Rhodes, irregular eyelets, couched boucle, Roumanian, Smyrna cross, bullion, lines of detached buttonhole, Portuguese knotted stem, chained cross, padded raised chain band, crested chain, French knots, needleweaving. 33 x 42 cm (13 x 17 in).

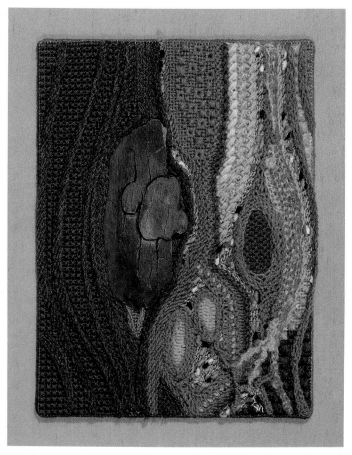

Sea of Cotton (author)—worked entirely in cotton threads. The sky is French knots, overlapping rows of fly, long legged chain and straight stitch. The sea is petal stitch and raised woven webs. The pelican is basketweave and layers of criss cross. The beak is wrapped pipe cleaners. The sails are cushion and variations of wheatsheaf. 58 x 68 cm (23 x 27 in).

Workbox and Needlebook (author)—expanding, hexagonal workbox,
heavily beaded areas with French knots, Rhodes stitch worked on irregular
shapes, basketweave stitch, padded applique and needleweaving.
Decorated with embroidered and beaded tassels and a hand twisted cord
through buttonholed loops. Needlebook edged with the binding stitch.
20 cm (8 in) dia. 15 cm (6 in) high. See page 83 for binding stitch.

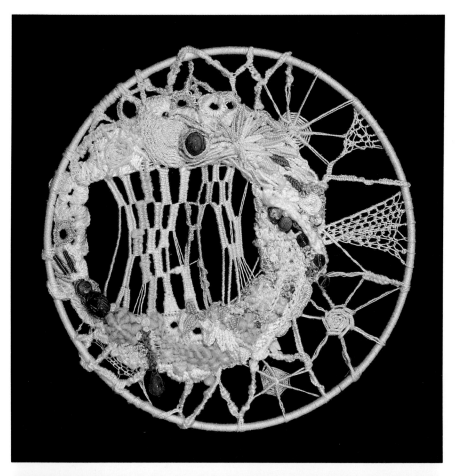

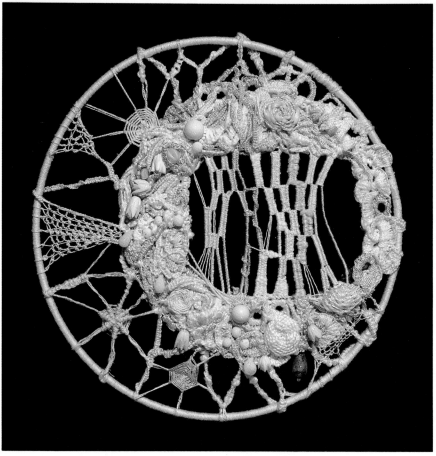

Crystal Cave (author)—double sided mobile, canvas embroidered firstly in a hoop then the edges cut, re-embroidered and needlewoven to a wrapped metal ring. The see-through central area was created by withdrawing weft canvas threads and needleweaving the remaining vertical threads. Square and buttonholed eyelets, raised stem and chain band, wrapped threads, woven webs, woven picots, French knot, needleweaving and beads. 21 cm (8 in) dia.

Above. *Malaysian Palms* (author)—inspired by a Malaysian holiday. Criss cross, basketweave, round, square and buttonholed eyelets, round Rhodes, woven webs, buttonholed rings and washers, bullion and French knot, beads, needleweaving, wrapped threads. Tassels are beaded, embroidered and needlewoven. Some tassel heads are covered beads, washers and lightweight wooden cylinders. 53 x 43 cm (21 x 17 in). Note criss cross variation, see page 23.

Above. *Rich and Exotic* (author)—pentagonal shoulder purse. Raised stem and chain band, cushion, Rhodes, leaf, basketweave, bullion and French knots, beads. Tassel heads are fabric covered lightweight wooden cylinders, embroidered and needlewoven. Shoulder cord is plaited with rouleaux and slubbed crochet cotton. 22 x 19 cm (9 x 7½ in). When not in use the purse hangs on a matching wall panel.

Left. *Lattice Mushroom* (author)—inspired by the exploding lattice fungus. Canvas is embroidered in buttonholed eyelets, ray, Rhodes, wheatsheaf, padded raised stem band, detached buttonhole. The edges were turned in and re-embroidered with buttonhole and needleweaving and applied to the box. The lattice effect is created by buttonhole stitched pipe cleaners. The box is divided within into three irregular shaped beaded and embroidered compartments. The 'spore' are fabric covered, beaded and embroidered triangles joined together by a needlemade chain cord. 19 cm (7½ in) dia. 17 cm (7 in) high.

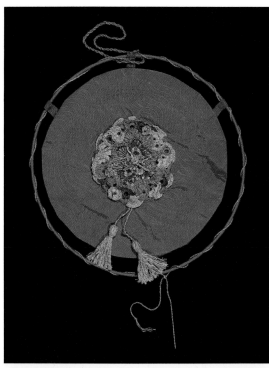

Left. *Rich and Exotic* (author)—drawstring purse clipped to a wrapped metal ring. When not in use the purse is hung as a wall decoration. Long legged chain, petal, buttonholed eyelets with re-embroidered edges, French knot, beads, needleweaving. After working the canvas in a hoop the edges were overlocked on the machine, cut and applied to fabric with buttonholed eyelets. 36 cm (14 in) dia.

Below. *Rich and Exotic* (author)—pentagonal shoulder purse. Five card shapes were covered with canvas embroidered with diamond eyelet, back stitch, three layers of criss cross variation, French knots, bullion and beads. They were joined together with the binding stitch. The shoulder cord is plaited with rouleaux, twisted cord and gold thread. Triangular fabric covered cardboard shapes are decorated with beads and embroidery. 18 cm (7 in) across. See page 83 for the binding stitch.

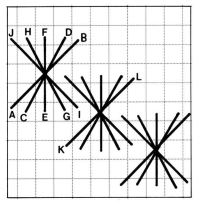

RHODES, HALF, HALF-DROPPED

As the name implies, work half a Rhodes stitch as in the diagram, working diagonally. Interlock each stitch into the previous one. This stitch must be worked over an even number of threads to obtain the half-dropped, interlocking effect.

▼ RICE OR CROSSED CORNERS

Work diagonal crosses over four threads square either by completing each cross as a separate unit or by running a row of half cross and returning back again with another row of half cross. When worked in alternating colours, particularly when the top colour is shiny, the crossed corners form an attractive diamond relief pattern. Cross the corners of the large diagonal crosses with a contrasting or matching thread of a lighter weight. Follow the instructions in Figures 2 and 3, which show diagonal half cross stitches crossing each corner of the large diagonal crosses.

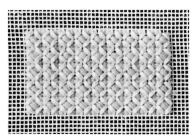

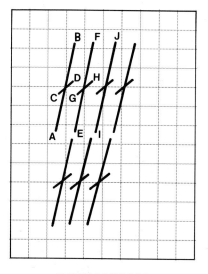

ROUMANIAN

This stitch can be worked over virtually any number of vertical threads and one diagonal thread, then tied in the middle with a tent stitch before being repeated. I suggest that the order of working in the diagram be followed so that when the subsequent rows are worked the needle will go down into the previous row (instead of up through it), which is easier to work and creates a neater finish.

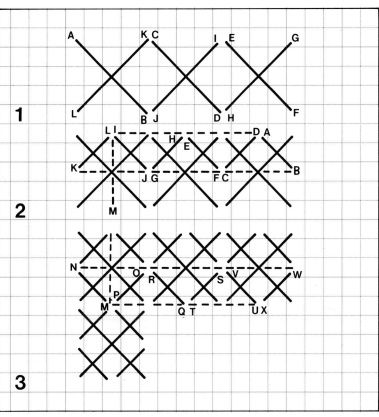

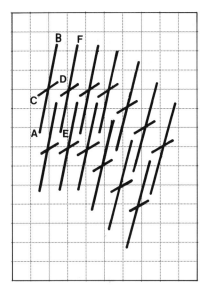

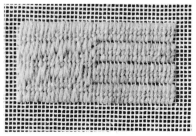

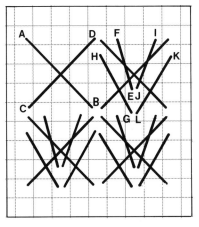

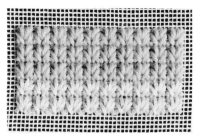

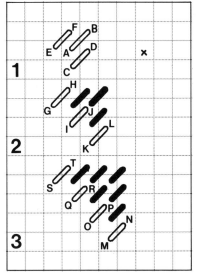

ROUMANIAN, INTERLOCKING

This is worked in the same manner as Roumanian except the subsequent rows are worked much closer together. This stitch, when worked in different lengths interlocked together, creates an interesting textured non-directional filler.

SMALL GROUNDING

This is an attractive filling stitch worked on a square of four threads. Work a diagonal cross A-B-C-D, come out at E, down into F, out at G, down at H, out at I, down into J, out at K and down at L. A little canvas may show between each stitch. If this effect is not desired, fill it with a small upright cross. This stitch can be worked in two colours by working the cross A-B-C-D in one colour and the top stitches E to L in a matching or contrasting thread.

TENT, BASKETWEAVE

Probably the most important stitch in canvas embroidery. For the best results and ease of working, the basketweave method is recommended. The stitch is so called because when worked correctly, it forms a woven basket pattern on the back of the work.

Starting at a point approximately 2 in. (5–6 cm) to the right of the first stitch (if this point is out of the edge of your work, snip the knot later and weave the end into the back of the work), work back stitches, following the diagram. Continue the back stitches in diagonal rows at every second intersection of threads. This method is recommended for all applications of tent stitch, no matter how small or large the space.

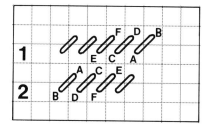

TENT, HORIZONTAL OR CONTINENTAL
Worked from right to left (Figure 1) or left to right (Figure 2)

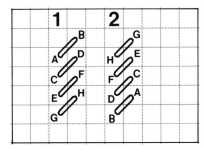

TENT, VERTICAL
Can be worked from top to bottom (Figure 1) or bottom up, as in Figure 2.

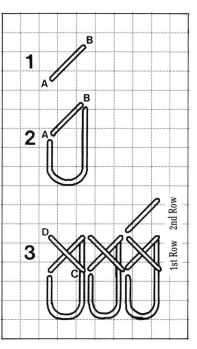

VELVET
This stitch is worked in horizontal rows from the bottom row upwards. Come out at A and down into B forming a half cross over two threads square. Come out at A and down into B again forming a loop with the thread. For an even row of loops work over a knitting needle held in place while working the row and then work the anchoring stitch C-D. Alternately, hold the loop down with the thumb while working C-D.

Velvet stitch may be left in even or uneven loops to form a rich knubbly effect. Or, when the area is completely worked, cut the loops with a very sharp pair of embroidery scissors and trim the pile to your requirements.

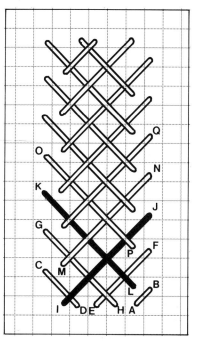

VICTORIA AND ALBERT HERRINGBONE
This herringbone stitch makes an interesting pattern and texture when used as a filler or to feature one row only. The starting stitches A to H fill the spaces to form a straight line, then the basic herringbone cross I-J-K-L is formed. Repeat the basic herringbone cross until the space is filled then work the filling stitches as per the diagram to form a straight line at the end.

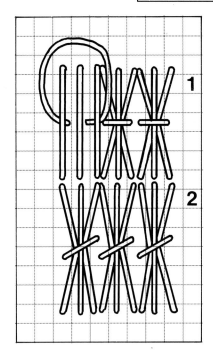

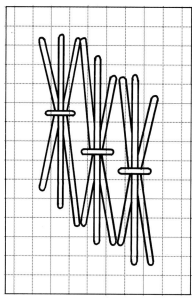

WHEATSHEAF VARIATION 1

Wheatsheaf need not necessarily be worked between two straight parallel lines, as shown in Figure 1. It can be varied by working freely between uneven, straight or curved lines, with the bar crossing each wheatsheaf placed at any position, not necessarily at the centre.

◀

WHEATSHEAF

Work three vertical straight stitches over an even number of horizontal threads and bring the needle out at the centre hole behind the middle stitch. Bring the thread around and over the three straight stitches to form a bar and take the needle back down into the same hole before proceeding to the next stitch. See Figure 1. To facilitate finding the centre hole, work the last straight stitch loosely, pulling it back with your fingernail to expose the hole and allow the needle to pass freely to the front. Secure the last stitch and pull back the first straight stitch with the needle to allow the needle to pass freely back down into the centre hole.

Threads of canvas will show through between the wheatsheafs. These can be covered by small back stitches over each thread of canvas, one straight stitch, or several French knots. Wheatsheaf can also be worked over an uneven number of horizontal threads but the tie stitch is then a diagonal stitch, as in Figure 2.

▲ WHEATSHEAF VARIATION 2

This is a very attractive filling or feature stitch variation of traditional wheatsheaf. Work five bars of satin stitch A-J as in the diagram. Bring the thread out at K and down into L to form the bar. Bring the thread out at F to commence the second wheatsheaf. Work horizontal rows from left to right and right to left. A contrasting or matching thread can then be used to fill the intervening spaces with a cross stitch, as shown in the diagram. ▼

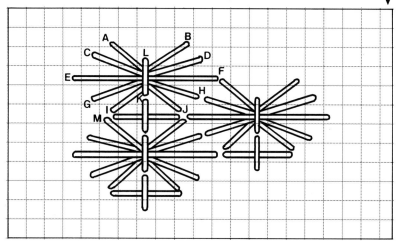

3

THE SAMPLER

Many of my generation cringe at the word 'sampler'. It brings memories of school where a rigid sampler of straight ruled lines was forced on sewing students. If you didn't do it perfectly you were often told to 'turn around, unpick it and do it again' even if you had to turn around five times for the same couple of inches! There was a great virtue in doing line after line of mathematically even stitches, imitating machine-like perfection.

I find it ironic that today machine embroiderers are 'humanising' machine embroidery to emulate asymmetrical, 'free' stitchery in direct opposition to what was required in the post-war era!

The *new* sampler can be a pleasurable and joyful experience having nothing to do with 'unpick it and do it again'. It is probably my childhood experiences of unpicking which have led me to devise ways of covering unwanted stitchery as padding for raised chain band or raised stem band. Furthermore, the sampler offers an outlet for experimentation and discovery — a chance to learn and have fun at the same time.

The sampler projects I suggest in the following pages are for those just starting out in canvas embroidery as a means of learning technique. However, even experienced embroiderers may find new pleasure in these projects by doing stitchery 'for its own sake'. You cannot learn to play the piano without practising scales, and you can't converse without an adequate vocabulary. Similarly, unless the embroiderer has a good and comprehensive vocabulary of stitches, accompanied by regular practice she/he will never be able to design and take full advantage of the range of possibilities for canvas work. Samplers are your 'scales'; so thread your needle, tie a knot and *enjoy...*

A Small Sampler

As a very first exercise to 'test the water', refer to Chapter 1 on Materials and Equipment and prepare a small hoop with canvas. Choose three or four stitches suggested under 'The First Project' and work these few stitches in different threads, sizes and colours. Practise working the stitches, enjoy the feel of the thread and the rhythm, movement and direction of the stitch. As you gain confidence proceed on to one of the projects set out in this chapter.

These small samplers can be made up into items as suggested in Chapter 6 on Project Ideas. The canvas itself does not need to cover the whole item to be made up. Indeed, adding a co-ordinating fabric to finish off the item, or ribbon edgings and bindings, enhances and complements the richness and texture of the canvas stitchery.

The First Project

Many beginning students, being somewhat overwhelmed by the large variety of stitches from which to choose, ask, 'What stitch should I start with?' For those who would like some direction in beginning the project I refer you to what is always the most difficult stitch — the *first* one! The actual difficulty has little to do with it: it's more the mental trauma of starting out.

My experience is that the following stitches give quick rewards in texture and covering the canvas:

Smyrna cross, cushion, Rhodes, ray or fan, fern, wheatsheaf, leaf, eyelet, tent, satin and French knots.

A good thread to start with is a canvas 'tapestry' thread or 5- or 8-ply knitting wool. Avoid crêpe at first as it is a little difficult to handle and tends to unravel and curl, making an uneven surface.

I have illustrated a sample first project in progress. As you will see on colour page *v*, the first stitch chosen was Smyrna cross over four threads square in a variegated 5-ply knitting wool, followed by Rhodes stitches over six threads square, having no regard for symmetry. These were followed by hound's tooth cross in a variegated knitting ribbon. After six stitches of hound's tooth were completed the ribbon was taken for a walk in satin stitch over two threads.

The picture shows the addition of ray or fan stitch in a nylon 5-ply knitting wool, square eyelet of different sizes in 5-ply crêpe, crossed cushion in tapestry wool crossed with No. 5 coton perle, fern stitch in the same wool as the Rhodes stitches, wheatsheaf in a soft knubbly 5-ply knitting wool, baby eyelets over two threads square in No. 5 knitting cotton and leaf stitch in a variegated soft 5-ply knitting wool.

The project continues with the addition of more wheatsheaf, irregular fan and ray, plaited cross, more baby eyelets and the addition of tent stitch and some small Smyrna crosses in No. 5 coton perle over two threads square.

To begin your own project, after choosing one of the stitches suggested for the first project and a suitable thread, work a group of this stitch on the canvas. When this has been done choose another thread and another stitch and work another group adjacent (that is, nearby but not necessarily touching) the first. Don't worry about filling in the spaces between the different stitches at this time, rather, practise working the stitch, enjoying the feel of the thread and the rhythm, movement and direction of the stitch.

Choose another colour and stitch and once again embroider adjacent or near to the first group, now thinking of interpreting the stitch as a line. That is, draw a straight or curved line on the canvas and work the stitch groups along the line. Continue embroidering your sampler in this manner. From time to time, or when you have some thread left over from working a particular stitch, start filling in the spaces left by the different stitches. I have a lot of fun using short lengths of leftover thread to fill in empty little areas. Filling empty areas with random stitches can produce very attractive effects and you'll surprise yourself with your ingenuity.

Continue trying out new stitches, working them in different threads, in groups of assorted size and scale according to the versatility of the particular stitch on which you are working. Work the stitch as a line, isolated as a single feature, or enlarged if possible, with no regard now for the blank areas of canvas left between stitch areas.

Refer to Chapter 2 under Random filling stitches, using this as a guide to assist you in choosing suitable stitches for the spaces left empty.

At some stage during the above procedure look in Chapter 6 on Project Ideas. According to what form you decide your finished product will take, determine how big your finished canvas work is to be and draw the appropriate shape on your canvas with a marking pen or pencil. Whilst working your projects you may care to try some special effects. In this case, refer to Chapter 5.

Some may care to retain their early projects or even ongoing ones in a reference book of stitchery and effects; others may feature these samplers as the front piece of a book cover or mounted as a wall panel.

The Second Project
STRIPES

Draw on a canvas a rectangle 6 in. x 4 in. (15 cm x 10 cm) and embroider each line in a different stitch. Continue these vertical and horizontal lines with new stitches and threads, eventually filling in the rectangle. The finished project can then be mounted onto an 8 in. x 6 in. (20 cm x 15 cm) board and framed with a padded top mount (see Chapter 7 on Mounting and Making Up). Another way of mounting the first and second projects is to cover a cylinder of cardboard or an empty tin, making a storage container. Again, refer to Chapter 7.

Compile a Permanent Reference File

Make canvas work 'pages' inserted into loose leaf plastic envelopes, which are then kept in a ring binder. This forms an invaluable dictionary for easy reference and choice of stitches.

1. Draw the shape of the page on your mounted canvas. Two should fit in a reasonably sized frame. It is not necessary to leave a seam allowance for this project.
2. Work groups of stitches on the canvas, leaving empty, unworked space between the groups. Each group of stitches should measure 1 ½ in. (4 cm) square or a 2 in. x 1 ½ in. (5 cm x 4 cm) rectangle. Use coordinating and contrasting colours for an integrated effect, once again using threads in different shades of each — dark, medium and light.
3. When you have completed your 'page', trim the edge a little and bind it with coloured ribbon or fabric on your sewing machine. Insert the finished canvas into the plastic envelope, which may then go into a ring binder with an attractive (embroidered!) cover.
4. To clearly label each stitch purchase small stickers or cut up a larger one and with the name of the stitch written on the sticker, stick it on the plastic envelope just under the appropriate group of stitches.

These pages will form an invaluable stitch reference for future projects, as the texture and effect of the stitch can be seen at a glance. Further improvements can be made to this stitch reference by photostating the actual stitched canvas page and drawing a stitch graph, showing how to work the stitch, either on top of the photostated group or to one side. Place the graph opposite the relevant canvas page in the folder.

Decorate your folder with a twisted cord around the side of the binder, and maybe a tassel or two hanging from the twisted cord place marker.

Because the reference file is in the form of a loose leaf ring binder you can always add more pages and handy notes as you enlarge your knowledge of creative canvas embroidery.

Keep a frame set up and handy for 'stitch doodling', or trying out different ideas or effects.

Divide the canvas into the proper sizes for the plastic insert sheets of your reference book and put these doodles into the book.

A 'chapter' of the book can be set aside for doodling, for photographs of interesting stitches or designs from other embroiderers' work, or your own and any other collectables which you find interesting and inspiring.

HELPFUL HINT

A knowledge of stitches and how they work is essential if one hopes to create on canvas what she/he imagines in the mind. The sampler, the early projects and the reference folder are recommended as exercises to enable a good working knowledge of the techniques of canvas embroidery.

4
DESIGN:
THE ARTISTIC TOUCH

As you begin to learn creative embroidery, you'll quickly discover that, though technique is a large part of what you're doing, there is another large part: design. Actually, deciding which of the two comes first is a 'chicken and egg' situation. Even I, as a teacher, waver between the two.

When I started learning creative embroidery I found that I couldn't limit myself to just mastering the stitch techniques. I needed to have in my mind the end result or design that I wanted to achieve. Soon, I found that when a need arose to achieve a certain effect, I investigated various techniques and stitches to achieve that.

Although I certainly acknowledge the other point of view, I now tend to think that a good understanding of stitches needs to come first. Having a solid working knowledge of basic techniques gives you the 'tool' with which to be creative, to invent new designs. This is what I recommend for 'raw beginners'. But, as always, the personality and desires of the individual stitcher are paramount; remember that the purpose of embroidery is to enjoy oneself and gain pleasure from the activity, *not* to let it all become a burden and a worry.

Elements of Design

Since the term 'design' may seem a bit abstract or daunting, I lay out here its main elements:

Line is the means by which we draw. This creates direction, be it vertical or horizontal, circular or enclosing a shape.

Shape is an area enclosed by a line.

Pattern is formed by repeating units of shape and line. It can be geometrically even or irregular, repetitive or asymmetrical. It can be striped or solid, circular or square. Pattern creates rhythm and movement for the eye that studies its results.

Colour is the sensation resulting from the stimulation of the eye by light waves. In embroidery, it is achieved using pigments and dyes.

Texture is the surface quality. It can be created by physically raising the surface of the subject by using padding, or by introducing objects like beads and pebbles. Texture is also affected by pattern and colour.

LINES AND STITCHES

Lines can be interpreted in canvas work by using canvas work stitches or stitches from other embroidery techniques. When deciding on which stitch to use to interpret a line, consider any and every stitch. Try forming lines using different stitches on your sampler or doodle canvas. For example a very fine and effective line is created by eyelet stitch over two threads square, placing the centre hole of each stitch as close to the line as it will go. The eyelet stitch is a particularly charming line stitch as a well-pulled eyelet hole dominates the stitch, taking the attention away from the square outline of each stitch. It's a pleasant surprise to find that a square stitch so successfully gives the appearance of a curved line. Sometimes you will have difficulty deciding which is the closest hole to the line; this comes down to the individual choice of the embroiderer. Trial and error is often the best method for coming to the final decision.

SHAPE AND STITCHES

A shape is the area created by lines. A shape can be geometric: round, triangular, square, rectangular. A shape can be free form: leaf, petal, ink blot, butterfly, cloud, fan. Shape is controlled by size, be it large, medium, small or microscopic. When choosing stitches to fill a shape, consideration should be given to the scale and texture of the desired effect. You'll also want to take into account the area of space to be covered, and whether a dominant or a subdued effect is required.

SECONDARY PATTERNS

In addition to the obvious patterns created by the stitches themselves — I call this the primary pattern — it is very important to learn how to make the most of the secondary patterns. Secondary patterns are created in canvas embroidery by the holes or perforations between stitches. An awareness of these patterns will assist in design. Therefore, achieving sharp, clear edges to your stitchwork becomes essential. The methods and specific stitch instructions I have laid out in this book are my recommendation for how to best achieve these perforations and stitch edges.

COLOUR

A basic knowledge of how colours are made up will enhance your embroidery.

There are three primary (or pure) colours: red, yellow and blue. All the other colours are mixtures of these three, with or without the addition of black and white.

Red represents warmth
Blue represents cold
Yellow is the lightest colour and represents brightness

When two primary colours are mixed together they produce a secondary colour: For example:

Red + blue = purple
Blue + yellow = green
Yellow + red = orange

Tertiary colours are made up by mixing a primary colour with a secondary colour :

Yellow + orange = yellow-orange
Red + orange = red-orange
Red + violet = red-violet
Blue + violet = blue-violet
Blue + green = blue-green
Yellow + green = yellow-green

The primary, secondary and tertiary colours form the twelve- part colour circle, which is an invaluable aid in understanding colour and how it works. The order of colours on the twelve-part colour circle, starting with primary yellow at the top of the circle and going clockwise, is:

yellow, yellow-orange, orange, red-orange, red, red-violet, violet, blue violet, blue, blue-green, green, yellow-green.

Illustrated in colour, page *xi*.

COLOUR CONTRASTS
1. Contrast of hue   Hue is the particular shade or tint of a given colour. The strongest expression of contrast of hue is

created when the primary colours red, yellow and blue are used together as a colour scheme. Strong colour contrasts are also created when red and blue/green are used together. Also when blue, yellow and violet, or yellow, green, violet and red, or violet, green, blue, orange and black are used together as colour schemes.

2. Light/dark contrast

The strongest expressions of light and dark are black and white. In between is the range of greys. The amount of black and white included in a pure colour or hue is referred to as the tone. The contrast of light and dark is therefore the contrast of tone.

3. Cold/warm contrast

The strongest expression of cold/warm contrast is red and green. Referring to the twelve-part colour circle, generally the colours yellow, yellow-orange, orange, red-orange, red and red-violet are referred to as warm. Yellow-green, green, blue-green, blue, blue-violet and violet are generally referred to as cool.

4. Complementary contrast

In the colour circle, complementary colours are diametrically opposite each other. Examples of complementary pairs are yellow/violet (which also represents an extreme light/dark contrast), blue/orange, red/green (extreme cold/warm contrast).

5. Harmonious contrast

A harmonious contrast is obtained when two or three colours adjacent to each other on the twelve-part colour circle are used together as a colour scheme. For example yellow/green of various shades and tones produces a pleasing colour scheme. Blue-green, blue/blue-violet or red/red-violet/violet are other harmonious combinations.

Nature is a wonderful source of creative colour schemes, particularly when studied at close range. For example, an ordinary-looking seashell, upon closer examination, may reveal purples and greens which at first glance are not apparent. Pebbles, rocks and stones aren't all brown and grey. I brought home a bottle of pebbles from a Mediterranean beach and on close inspection discovered nine different greens, orange, eight browns and fawns, cream, beige, grey and beautiful thin lines of red/violet.

A photograph of Mt. Olga in Australia's Northern Territory at a certain time of day and year contained numerous tones of red/violet through to blue-violet and blue, green trees, many shades of red, the brown and orange of the sand, a blue-grey sky containing white clouds tinged with mauve/pink.

Many colours are found in one leaf. Autumn abounds as inspiration for colour. Sea and shore, rainforests, landscapes and the seasons are endless sources of inspiration and colour moods.

Observe these phenomena and follow your own individual intuitive colour preferences, which in my experience produce the most successful colour schemes.

For a deeper understanding of colour I recommend a book called *The Elements of Colour* by Johannes Itten, published by Van Nostrand Reinhold in the USA, 1987.

TEXTURE

Many artists choose the medium of embroidery because of the marvellous textures which are unique to this form. The first reaction of a person admiring embroidery is often to touch it, running one's fingers across surfaces ranging from smooth to rough, even rocky!

Texture is heightened by relating one area of texture to another: for example, an area of bullion knots or Rhodes stitch looks more raised and textured when worked adjacent to an area of tent stitch, cushion stitch or other flat stitches. Rough appears rougher if contrasted by an area of smooth; different weights of texture add interest.

Texture can be symmetrical, asymmetrical, dotted, striped, ridged, random, shiny, dull.

PROJECT IDEA

Using pieces of fabric, house paint colour cards, pieces of coloured paper or magazine cutouts, make a collage colour wheel in colours as close as possible to the pure colours. This exercise will heighten your awareness of the relationships between the colours.

PROJECT IDEA

Select one of the above colour contrasts and, using pieces of coloured paper, paint, threads and yarns, bring together in a group one of the above colour contrasts. For example, take the strongest cold/warm combination of red and green. Bring together as many reds and greens as you have on hand: you will be amazed to see how many shades and tones there are.

These effects create visual as well as tactile texture.

CONTRAST OF TEXTURE

This can be achieved by using the following methods:—

1. Inverted stitches next to raised or flat stitches. I classify inverted stitches as those which form the flattest effect on canvas, such as eyelets with well-pulled eyelet holes or withdrawn threads.

2. Added objects like beads, shells and bark.

3. Other embroidery techniques worked on canvas like:

Needleweaving — using a piece of wool or yarn you've selected, make a long straight stitch between two points and then buttonhole it. Another method of needleweaving is to make two or more long straight stitches and weave backwards and forwards, under and over the straight or laid stitches.

Pulled thread — in this technique of embroidery the threads of the ground fabric, in this case canvas threads, are compressed by pulling the stitches tightly, thereby creating holes which form attractive patterns.

Withdrawn thread embroidery combined with needleweaving — to work this technique threads of the canvas ground fabric, prior to embroidering, are first cut and removed from the ground material. Then, instead of using yarn or wool to make long straight stitches to form the core of needleweaving, use the canvas ground threads and follow the needleweaving technique described above.

Surface Stitches such as the stem, chain, Portuguese knotted stem and many others.

Appliqué flat or raised.

4. Holes cut in the canvas. The edge of the hole can be overlocked with buttonhole stitch or binding stitch. Interesting pieces of material or embroidery can be placed behind the hole to create a second layer and dimension.

5. Raised and detached stitches such as raised chain, raised stem, buttonhole.

To summarise, when deciding on the way to fill a shape ask yourself the following questions:

• Is a dominant or subdued effect required?

• Is a non-directional textured effect required?

• What level of texture is required?

• Will the secondary pattern dominate and distract?

This may seem like a lot of difficult questions to ask yourself but they are included for consideration when special effects are required. I recommend that you generally choose stitches which you

PROJECT IDEA

• Prepare a tray containing different objects of varying texture such as a feather, or bark, pebbles, rough stones, and different fabrics like satin, suede, slubbed linen or polyester. Close your eyes and feel each article on the tray, endeavouring to identify the piece being examined. This exercise helps heighten your awareness of tactile texture. Try to think of words to describe the way the objects feel (this may be difficult at first as we often rely heavily on our eyesight; our tactile sense is largely dormant).

• As another exercise in examining texture, make rubbings of textured objects such as a tree trunk, a leaf or a coin. Using a fine piece of writing paper and charcoal or very soft pencils, place the paper on the surface and rub the paper with the pencils or charcoal. This will create areas of pattern formed by the texture of the surface being rubbed.

intuitively like; if you have trouble deciding, then refer to the above self-analysis.

Choosing the Right Stitch

I have grouped these stitches into categories according to the effect that is achieved. For example, if in doubt as to what stitch to use to embroider the details of a flower, you might look under 'circles'. Be aware, however, of some of the variations. A stitch such as rice or Norwich is worked on a square but its effect is that of a diamond. You will discover these twists as you experiment!

SQUARE

Cross — diagonal, cross — double, cross — hound's tooth, cross — plaited, cross — Smyrna, cross — Smyrna variation, cross — squared and interlaced, cushion — crossed, cushion — mosaic, eyelet, fan or ray, Italian two-sided, leviathan, leviathan 1 and 2, Norwich or waffle, petal, Rhodes, rice or crossed corners, small grounding.

HORIZONTAL SECONDARY PATTERN

Cross — diagonal half or satin, cross — long legged, cross — oblong, Gobelin, Gobelin — encroaching, oblique — horizontal, Parisian, Victoria and Albert herringbone, wheatsheaf variation 2.

NON-DIRECTIONAL FILLER AND TEXTURE

Brick, bullion knot, criss cross, cross — interlocking and tied, cross — vertical or upright, Ghiordes knot, link surface, random filling stitches, Roumanian — interlocking, tent.

DIAGONAL SECONDARY PATTERN

Cashmere, cross — large double filler, cross — plaited and interlaced, cushion — crossed, diagonal, leaf — diagonal, Milanese, oblique — horizontal, Oriental, Rhodes — half.

DIAMOND

Cross — diamond, diamond patterned fillings, eyelet — diamond, Hungarian, leaf, leaf — diagonal, Norwich or waffle, rice or crossed corners.

CIRCLES AND HALF-CIRCLES

Eyelet circles — buttonholed, eyelet — half-circles, eyelet — buttonholed, eyelet — half or fantail, eyelet — round, petal.

VERTICAL

Fern, fishbone, wheatsheaf, wheatsheaf variation 1.

The Practicalities of Design

Design is not only an artistic issue; it is also a practical one. The chair is of no use if it doesn't hold together. Likewise, if you intend to make a cushion but end up with a canvas in the shape of a lampshade, you need to spend a little more effort in the design process. I suggest these guidelines to assist you as you design:

• Where is your work going to be used? Decide this before beginning to design.
• Is it going on a wall? If so, is the space large or small, high or low, to be looked at from a distance, or close up as in a small hallway?
• Will it become a cushion?

Will it belong to a single chair, a two-seater sofa, a three-seater lounge chair or on the floor? Should the cushion be large or small? Is the size compatible with the chair or floor on which it is to be placed?
• When the crucial decision as to the use of the article has been made, consider materials and threads that are relevant to that use. For example, a cushion would be most uncomfortable with large wooden beads sewn into the embroidery. On the other hand, a cushion with lovely, big, wooden beads on it might intentionally discourage people from leaning on it if its use is for decorative purposes only. Similarly, you will want to choose suitable materials and threads if the work is to be laundered, or if it will be used only as a decoration such as a wall hanging.

Some people will tell you that they can't plan a design and that they just like to start with an idea they have in their head. This is called intuitive embroidery and can be a lot of fun.

You do need to be aware of problems that may arise, however. The embroiderer often reaches a point where she/he is unable to finish the embroidery because of a design fault which cannot be corrected midstream through the project. Should this happen to you, don't despair. If you have no ideas at this stage for where your work is going to be used, approach the project as a learning experience, an exercise for exploring stitches, effects and other experiments. No matter how 'way out' they may at first appear to be, this is your chance to try any new ideas and inspirations because you aren't constricted by any specific goal or plan. These projects can be very rewarding.

Designing for Canvas

Designing for canvas embroidery differs from designing for other embroidery techniques. The open grid of the canvas limits the number of stitches that can be worked in a given shape or space. It is therefore necessary when drawing the design lines that will enclose the space or shape to be worked to leave sufficient space so that the stitches can effectively be worked. The smaller the space, the fewer your options when it comes to choosing stitches and other decorative possibilities. If the space is very small, your only choice may be the tent stitch.

The following exercise is an illustration.

EXERCISE A

1. Using a pencil, draw a square on large-grid graph paper as if it were a piece of canvas, enclosing twelve lines square. The enclosed grid will resemble a mesh of canvas that is twelve threads square, the lines of the graph paper represent the threads of the canvas. (I find 5-mm-square graph paper suitable.) Divide the square into smaller squares by hand-drawing lines in between the lines on the graph, two lines or threads apart. Refer to Figure 1. Draw stitches in the spaces. It will be seen that if stitches are used which cover two threads square (such as Smyrna cross, ray, cushion or small eyelet), then thirty-six units of such stitches will fit in the area.

2. Draw another square the same size on the graph paper again enclosing twelve threads square. This time divide the square into smaller squares, four lines or threads square. Stitches requiring four threads square are those like Smyrna cross, Rhodes, ray, Italian two-sided, eyelet and cushion. Only nine units of these stitches will fit in the diagrammed area. Refer to Figure 2.

3. Draw another square and divide it into diamonds four threads apart. This is done by marking with a dot the space four lines apart on each outside line of the square, then joining the dots as shown in Figure 3 the dots marked A to L. Twelve complete diamond-shaped stitches will fit in the space, stitches like diamond patterned fillings, diamond eyelet and diamond cross.

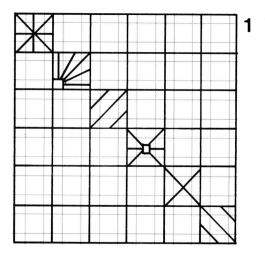

1

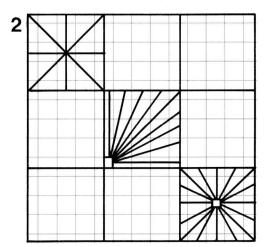

2

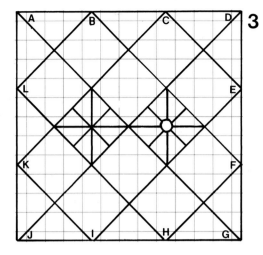

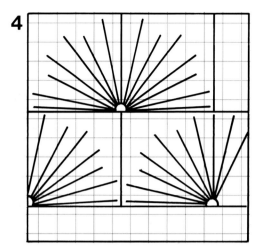

4. Draw another square and divide it into the shape of the stitch you now decide to work. For example, fantail is worked on a rectangular shape ten vertical by five horizontal threads. As can be seen in Figure 4 only one complete fantail, half of another and three-quarters of a third fantail will fit in the space.

EXERCISE B

As another method of finding out how many units of stitches will fit into a given area, work all the basic stitches in the sampler format (see Chapter 3) and enter them in your permanent reference file. You can also draw squares in pencil straight onto your doodle or sampler canvas, enclosing twelve threads square. Follow the directions in Exercise A but instead of drawing the stitches, work them on canvas. This will take longer than Exercise A but is an excellent way of practising the stitches while working out their design potentials.

DESIGN AND SCALE

Design for canvas should be basically simple without much detail. The stitches need space in which to be executed to give their best effect. If there isn't enough space, or if there is too much detail cluttering up what area there is, your choice of stitches will be very limited, and the many possibilities for developing textural richness will be inhibited. Do not over-work your designs and try to be free and open. Later, using filling stitches and effects you can intensify the space as you wish.

Scale is an important consideration in design and is affected in canvas work by:

- the choice of grid size
- the size and nature of the stitch chosen to fill the canvas, and
- the weight and thickness of thread chosen to work the stitches — to a certain extent this is controlled by the mesh size of the chosen canvas, but not altogether. For example, a thin shiny thread might be chosen to work on a large mesh canvas. This thin shiny thread can be doubled to give more cover of the canvas ground, but when worked will give a lighter more open-work effect than a very thick wool worked in the same stitch. This choice

of thread affects the scale of the work.

As can be seen from the above exercises, designing for canvas embroidery requires an understanding of:

- the number of threads available to work stitches, and
- the scale of the work.

These choices offer you further opportunities to make your design creation unique and individual to you.

Designing for a Wall Panel

I have repeated this advice in Chapter 7 on Mounting and Making Up. It is easier to design a wall panel working backwards from the size of the finished panel. For those who wish to save time and effort in mounting the work it is an excellent idea to purchase from your local framer light-weight acid-free masonite cut in standard sizes. Buy one board for the work to be mounted on and a larger one for the backboard.

A Final Word

Understanding design is an exercise that occurs over a period of time. Despite all the confusion, it usually happens that one day everything suddenly falls into place. Until that time, and it varies from person to person, *action* must be taken in several ways: exercises, observing and being aware of things around you. Practical note keeping I find is one of the most important tools. Collect photographs, pictures from magazines, drawings and sketches, and objects such as leaves, shells, pieces of bark, feathers and fabrics of any kind and colour. This makes you *aware* of the compositions, shapes and textures found in nature as well as in all of humankind's wondrous designs.

Once these attitudes — taking action in a practical way, becoming more aware and observant of the world around you — become part of your everyday life, you will be amazed at how your appreciation and wonder of everything you come into contact with will be enriched. Whether you actually design an embroidery or anything else, becomes almost secondary.

Design is a heightened sense of awareness of the way things are made and how they work — be it a can opener that works properly or a chair that is functional and comfortable but not very pleasing to the eye. In the same way, a chair which seems very attractive, has lovely lines and beautiful upholstery might be very uncomfortable to sit in or difficult to get out of. One person may prefer the comfortable, functional chair; another may not care or notice the discomfort of the 'uncomfortable' and difficult to climb out of, but aesthetically pleasing chair. Once again, design is a matter of individual choice. The fact that one is *aware* of the difference indicates an understanding and appreciation of design.

Two books that I highly recommend to embroiderers are *Design in Embroidery*, by Kathleen Whyte, published by B.T. Batsford Limited in Australia and the U.K. and *The Art of the Needle*, by Jan Beaney, published by Simon and Schuster in Australia in 1989. In any case I suggest you invest in a basic book on design and colour or borrow one from your local library. A small study of books will increase your knowledge and awareness.

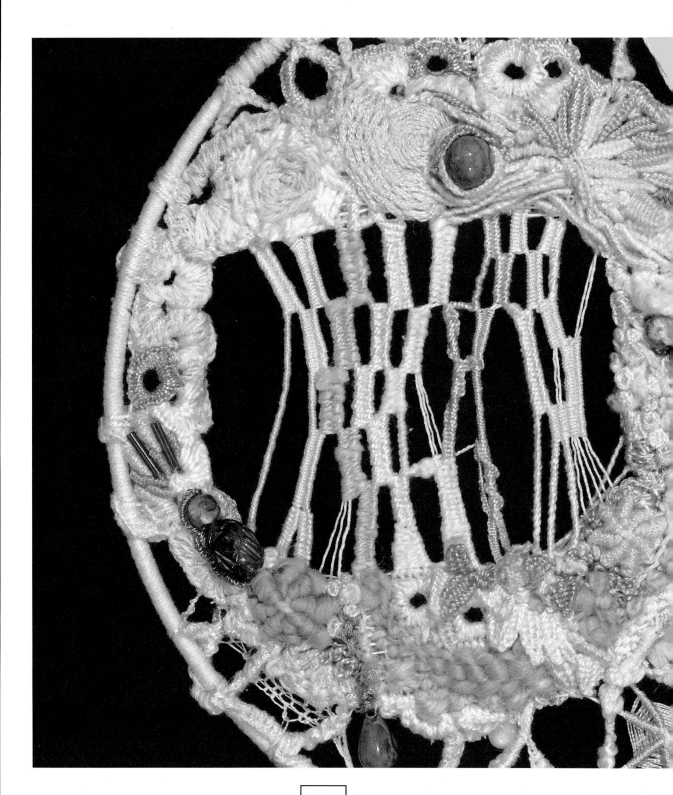

5

CREATING TEXTURE AND SPECIAL EFFECTS

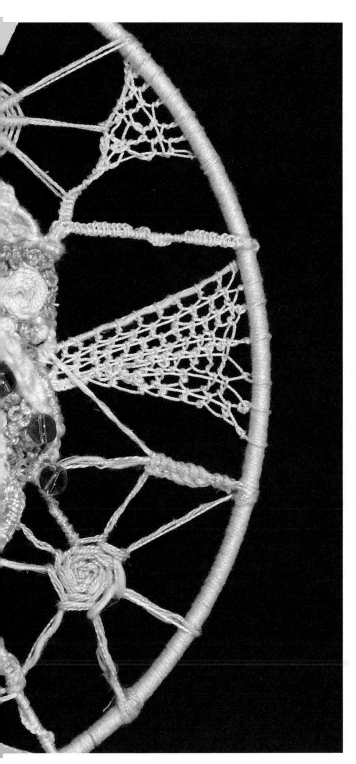

*T*he stitches set out in this chapter are not traditional to canvas embroidery, but are 'borrowed' from other types of embroidery work. I find them invaluable by combining them with canvas work stitches to create texture and special effects. These stitches can be combined with random texture to fill spaces between stitch areas, which I find enhances the adjoining stitches.

Beads can also be used to add further depth and dimension. It's great fun bead-swapping with friends, and finding beads of new colours and shapes in the most unexpected places — old jewellery, for example. Opportunity shops sometimes have old necklaces, or old garments laden with beads. An elderly neighbour or relative might have some tucked away in a drawer. Failing these sources, you can resort to buying packets of beads from wholesale and retail outlets.

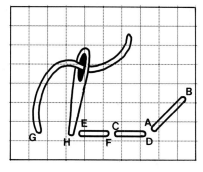

BACK

This is a versatile sewing stitch used in garment making as well as embroidery. It can be used for joining seams as well as decorating spaces of canvas which show between some canvas stitch units. Two or more back stitches worked one on top of the other serve as firm anchoring stitches. Come out at A, down into B and out at C. Repeat this movement for each stitch.

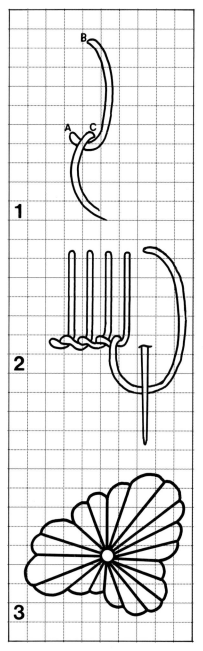

may be worked next to each other or partly on top of the previous row to form a raised effect. The nature of the looped stitch creates a space at the loop through which canvas shows. If this is not the desired effect, first work a row of straight stitches (described under Padded Raised Chain Band and Raised Stem Band later in this chapter) and work the buttonhole stitch over the top. The buttonhole stitch is very attractive worked as round or irregular-shaped eyelets.

BUTTONHOLE

Bring thread out at A and down into B, forming a loop. Hold the loop with your thumb and pass the needle through to come out at C. Pull the thread firmly while holding it again with the thumb to form the loop for the next stitch. Repeat. Buttonhole stitch can be worked on a straight or curved line, with the stitches forming even parallel rows or uneven wavy rows. The rows

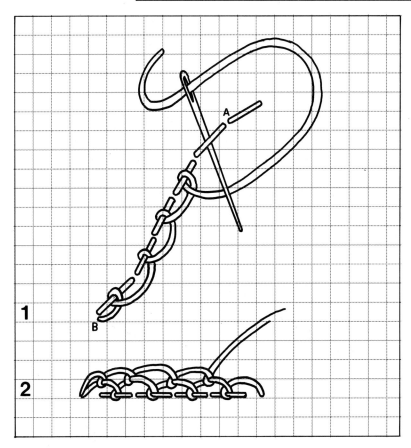

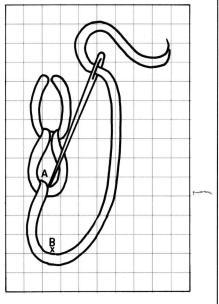

CHAIN STITCH

Bring the thread out at A and form a loop holding it down with the thumb. Take the needle down into A coming out at B. Tighten the loop by gently pulling the thread. The tail of the next stitch stabilises the loop of the first. Repeat. This stitch can be used freely as a space filler, as a line, or as a detached chain for feature stitches.

DETACHED BUTTONHOLE

This is a very effective free-line stitch that can be worked on curved or straight lines as well as encircling a shape, forming a raised collar effect. First, work a row of back stitch over two threads of canvas, commencing at A. Bring the thread out at the last stitch at B and begin the buttonhole stitch, using the back stitch as the grounding. Do not go through the canvas. To work a second and consecutive row it is not necessary to work in the same direction as the first row. Make an anchoring stitch at the back of the work, bring the thread out at the same hole as the last stitch and work a row of buttonhole back over the top of the previous row.

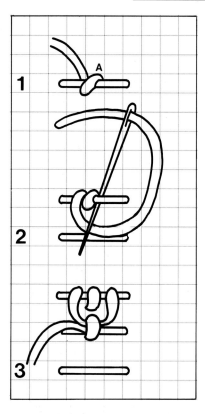

RAISED CHAIN BAND

A foundation of bars must be worked first, two canvas threads apart. If the thread being worked as the chain band is very thick, spread the bars further apart. If using a boucle or thick bubbly thread of uneven width, the bars would be better worked with an ordinary tapestry or knitting wool for ease of passage through the canvas. This is an excellent stitch in which to use the lovely boucle and uneven knitting threads available on the market.

To work the raised chain stitches come out at A, bring the thread over the top of the bar and then under the bar on the left-hand side to come out above the bar again adjacent to A but not going through the canvas. Make a loop with the thread, holding it down with the thumb, and take the needle from the top of the bar, under the bar and forming a chain stitch. Pull firmly but not too tightly in order to form the completed raised chain on the bar. At no time does the thread

pass through the canvas surface until the last anchoring stitch is made.

COUCHING

Couching is very useful for applying thick knubbly wools that cannot pass through the canvas as needed for traditional stitchery. The choice of the couching or tying thread is as important as the thread to be couched, as so many effects can be obtained by using different threads.

The colour photograph on page x shows a knubbly homespun, sewn or couched down with small straight couching stitches. To fill an area, lie the next row parallel to the first either matching or varying the positions of the couching stitches.

Attractive effects can be obtained by couching a line of thread parallel to a previous line, then varying the distance away from the line to create an area of canvas, which can be filled with traditional canvas work stitches, French knots, beads, and so forth.

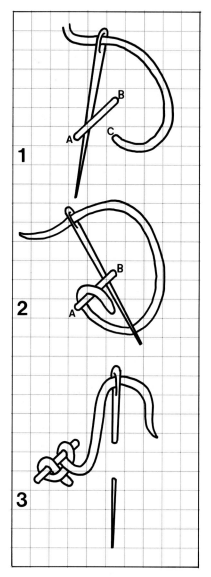

DOUBLE OR PALESTRINA KNOT

To make a knotted line with a beaded effect, double knot or Palestrina is a very useful and attractive line stitch. Worked in rows by itself or in conjunction with other stitches, it can also be used as a filling stitch. It resembles raised chain band except each chain has its own band A-B, as shown in the diagram.

Bring thread out at A and down into B, forming the foundation bar. Come out at C and thread the needle behind A-B. Make a loop with the thread, holding it with the thumb. Take the needle back down under A-B forming a chain stitch. Repeat. The effect of the knotted line will vary according to the thickness of thread used. Double or Palestrina knot stitch is very effective for decorating seams.

FRENCH KNOT

To work French knots on fabric in a frame, bring thread out at A holding it with the left hand (left handers please reverse). With the right hand hold the needle on top of the thread as shown in the diagram. With the left hand bring the thread forward over the needle and wind it round the needle once, as shown in Figure 2. Still holding the thread firmly with the left hand, point the needle down into the next hole in the canvas at B. The tension of the thread held by your left hand will control the size of the knot. When the thread is held tightly a tight knot will result. When the thread is held firmly but not too tightly a larger knot will result. However, if the thread is held too loosely a loop can form that is very difficult to undo; but the looped effect can also be very attractive.

Variations of the French knot can be created by winding the thread around the needle two, three or more times before pulling the thread through.

If an error is made in working the French knot it is very difficult to unpick. The easiest way to overcome this is to firmly pull the thread from the back, pulling the unwanted stitch through to the back so you can work another one on top.

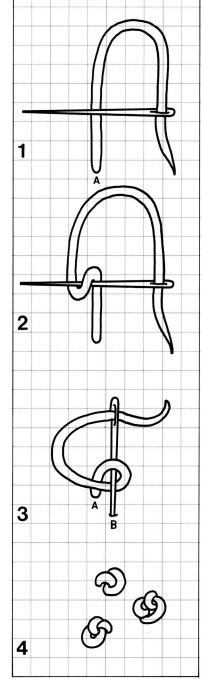

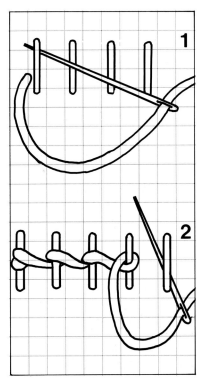

RAISED STEM BAND

As in raised chain band, a foundation of bars first needs to be worked two canvas threads apart, either horizontally, vertically or diagonally. Then work parallel rows of stem stitch over two bars using the bars as 'fabric' and not stitching through the canvas. When the end of a row is reached, take the thread into the canvas and come out at the hole next to the first commencing stitch of the following row. This stitch can also be worked backwards and forwards after an anchoring stitch has been taken into the back of the work. However, be sure that the stem stitches are not reversed when working in the opposite direction unless that is the desired effect. That is, when each row is worked in the opposite direction and care is not taken to reverse the working of the stem stitch, the effect produced will look like a knitting stitch.

▲ STEM

This stitch, which is traditionally not a canvas work stitch, is very attractive when used for shading. It can be worked in straight lines using the horizontal and vertical holes of the canvas, or in free curved lines.

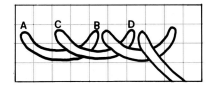

Raised Areas

Padding is a means of forming attractive raised areas that can then be covered with fabric or stitchery. There are two techniques I recommend for padding: wool and yarn padding, and felt padding. I strongly recommend that these techniques of padding and raised stitches be incorporated in your sampler projects so that you can see their beauty and potential as soon as possible. They are not difficult to do and offer quick rewards.

Padded raised chain band and raised stem band

WOOL AND YARN PADDING

Padding with two or more layers of wool or yarn is very quick and effective. This forms a base over which raised stitches can be worked, such as raised chain band, raised stem band and detached buttonhole. This form of padding can also be worked over areas of undesired stitching that you don't wish to unpick. If the stitching to be covered is fairly raised it may only be necessary to work one row of straight padding stitches prior to commencing the raised stitches.

PADDED RAISED CHAIN BAND AND RAISED STEM BAND

Starting about 3 in. (8 cm) away (refer to Chapter 2 under How to start and finish off) with a knot on the end of the thread, go down into the canvas coming up through the canvas to the area to be padded. Work straight vertical stitches until the area to be padded is covered. There is no point working satin stitches because the padding stitches will not be seen.

The next layer of padding to be worked on top of the vertical straight stitches will form the horizontal bars on which the raised chain or raised stem band is to be worked. The photograph shows the horizontal bars worked in every second hole of the canvas to allow room for the stitch to fit properly. If a very thick wool is to be used for the raised stem or raised chain band the bars should still be worked every second hole but, to compensate, a bar or two can be skipped when working the stitches on top.

To work the top row bring the thread out at the top of the padded area, one or two threads from the left to allow for the chain stitch to sit properly. Work raised chain band or raised stem band. At the bottom of the padded area, when each row has been completed, take an anchoring stitch at the back of the canvas. Bring the thread up to the top of the padded area to commence the second vertical row. Depending on the thickness of the wool leave one, two, three or more vertical threads between the rows of raised chain band to allow for the stitches to sit properly. If an open effect is required with the padding showing through, perhaps in a matching or contrasting colour or thread, leave as many horizontal canvas threads as desired between rows to create the desired effect.

FELT PADDING

Another form of padding is to stitch three graduating layers of felt one on top of the other, as follows:

1. Cut out a piece of felt slightly larger than the shape to be covered.
2. Cut a second piece of felt slightly smaller than the first piece.
3. Cut a third piece of felt smaller than the second.
4. First, apply the smallest piece of felt with small hem stitches to the centre of the area to be padded.
5. Following this, apply the second piece of felt in the same manner over the top of the first piece.
6. Finally, apply the largest

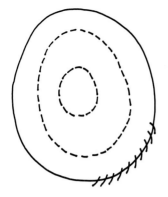

piece on top of the other two, using small hem stitches at the edge of the padded area.

Felt padding is suitable for covering with raised chain band, raised stem band, detached buttonhole, couching and appliqué fabric such as suede, leather and any other non-fraying fabric.

6

SOMETHING TO SHOW FOR YOURSELF: PROJECT IDEAS

*I*nstructions are given in this chapter for the following project ideas:

- cushion
- dice shaker
- eyeglass case
- notebook cover
- paperweight
- napkin rings, using instructions for a cylinder

The techniques and ideas that go into making these projects are transferable to literally hundreds of other ideas. There's no limit where imagination and creativity are involved.

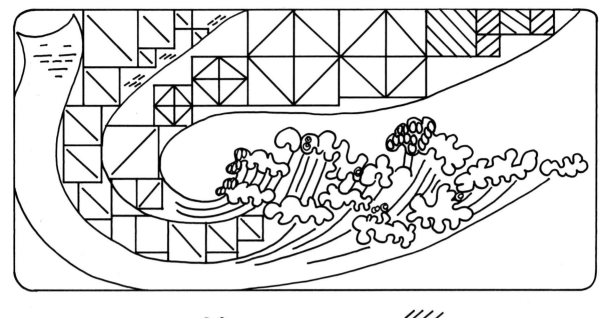

☰ Hungarian	⊙⊙⊙ French Knots	⫽ Mosaic
⊠ Crossed Cushion	⟋⟋⟋ Bullion Knots	⫽⫽ Tent

Cushion

This cushion is shown in miniature and makes a lovely pincushion. It can also be enlarged for soft furnishings and bedecked with tassels. As shown on the pattern and in the made-up pincushion, suggested stitches are Hungarian, crossed cushion, bullion knots, mosaic, tent and French knots.

Dice Shaker

A small cylindrical shape, such as a plastic pill bottle or a clear plastic spice or stock cube container, when covered with canvas embroidery makes an attractive dice shaker.

Using your own choice of stitches (or you can refer to the second project from Chapter 3), follow the directions in Chapter 7 for covering a cylinder.

Eyeglass Case

The pattern for the eyeglass case is illustrated here. If the size specified is too small or large for your eyeglasses make your own pattern, leaving sufficient space for the eyeglasses to fit comfortably.

Stitches you can use include buttonholed eyelets, raised stem band executed in a thick bubbly wool, and a background of rice stitch.

The case is comprised of an envelope of two pieces of canvas and is lined inside with a thin fabric. The sides can be joined with the binding stitch or just sewn together, the seam concealed with a twisted cord or a row of double or Palestrina knots. A third alternative is binding.

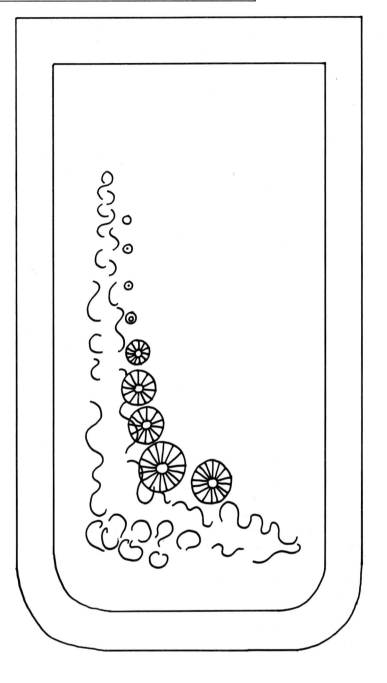

Notebook Cover, Wall Hanging or Box Lid

The 'two oysters' design can be used to make a notebook cover, a wall hanging or a box lid. Instructions are given to make a notebook cover as follows:

1. Work your own design or trace and work the 'two oysters' pattern. Objects such as shells can be attached to the canvas.

2. Make up the front cover of the notebook folder according to the directions for the recessed mounting or picture frame method (see Chapter 7). However, don't seal the fourth side until the gusset has been inserted and glued into place.

3. Cut out two pieces of fabric 1½ in. (4 cm) longer than the back cover *plus* ½ in. (12 mm) seam allowance all around, as in Figure 3.

4. Machine sew around three sides of the fabric, leaving one of the small ends open. The back cover of the notebook is to be inserted into this envelope. First, fold back and glue or sew on the inside back cover. Refer to Figure 4.

5. Insert the gusset between the recessed mounting of the inside front and glue into place.

6. Conceal the exposed seams by gluing a hemmed piece of fabric over the gusset.

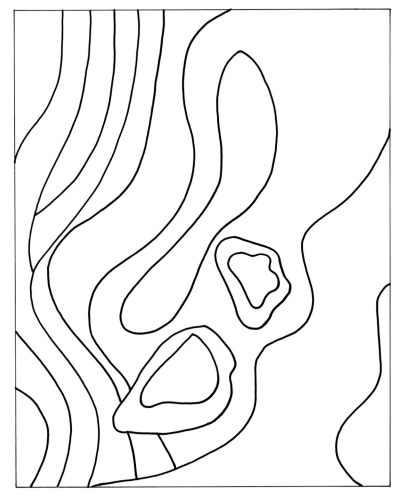

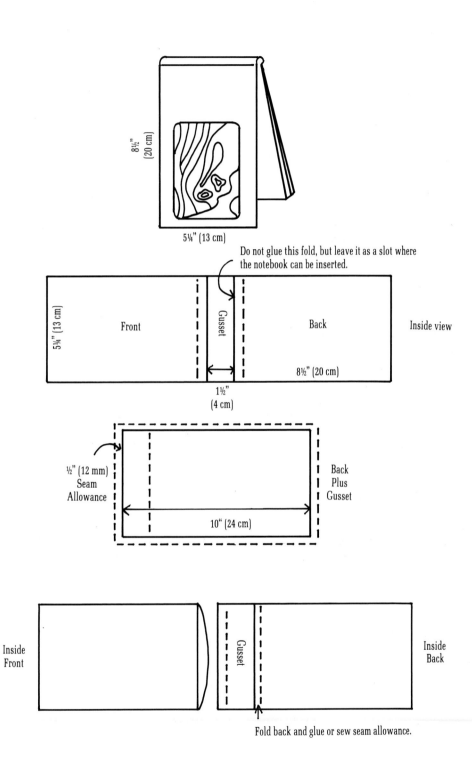

8½"
(20 cm)

5¼" (13 cm)

Do not glue this fold, but leave it as a slot where
the notebook can be inserted.

5¼" (13 cm)

Front

Gusset

Back

Inside view

8½" (20 cm)

1½"
(4 cm)

½" (12 mm)
Seam
Allowance

Back
Plus
Gusset

10" (24 cm)

Inside
Front

Gusset

Inside
Back

Fold back and glue or sew seam allowance.

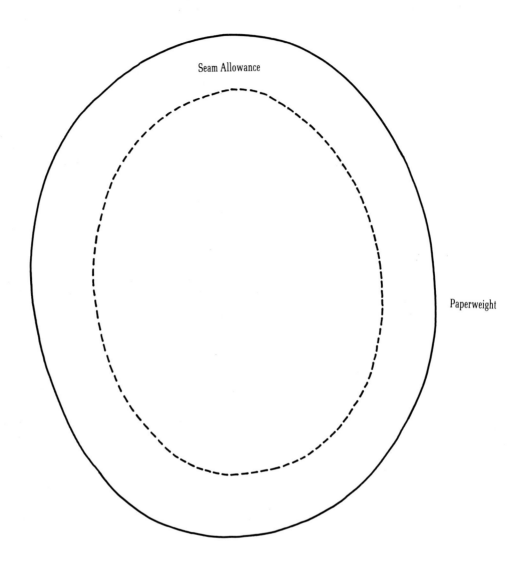

Seam Allowance

Paperweight

Paperweight

A decorative paperweight is an ideal opportunity to display the rich, textured results of canvas embroidery. Found objects and unusual beads and threads, incorporated with canvas stitches, will produce a very attractive ornament. A pattern guide is given here, but the size will depend on the size of the pebble you choose; the pattern will therefore need to be adjusted. Allow extra canvas to cover the pebble as the buildup of threads at the back of the work will act as padding, making the area to be covered larger.

When the canvas work is complete, leave a seam allowance of 1 in. (2.5 cm). Machine stitch two rows of zigzag or serpentine stitch around the edge to prevent fraying. Gather up the canvas around the pebble. Finish off the bottom of the paperweight by gluing or sewing a piece of suede or fabric over the raw edges. If using a fabric that frays, turn in the edges before gluing or sewing it into place.

This article is suitable for working in a hoop — refer to the instructions in Chapter 1.

Working in a Hoop

When designing work to be done in a hoop, design within the circular shape of the frame as the eyes will automatically relate to the circular edge whilst working. However, if you wish to design a square or other shape to work on a hoop, draw the edge of the shape onto the canvas to ensure that the desired proportions and scale of the article come within the frame's perimeter.

EXERCISE — SMALL SHAPES

Materials required:
• embroidery hoop
• one or more bottles of selected, colour-graded beads and sequins in compatible sizes
• circular canvas prepared for working in the hoop
• threads — to include a variety of thicknesses in wool, knitting and crochet cottons, coton perle, stranded, and so forth in colours that appeal to you and blend with your inspirations and ideas; also including a range of different tones of one colour with a harmonious or contrasting colour, plus creams, whites, off-whites, bones and neutrals. For example:
• soft pinks *or* apricots, harmonising with soft browns, cream and off-whites
• soft greens contrasting with soft pinks, creams and off-whites
• soft greens harmonising with yellow, cream and off-white.

PROJECT IDEAS

Use your imagination! Embroidery can serve both useful and decorative purposes. Here are some more suggestions:

- address book cover
- blender cover
- box top
- Christmas cards
- coat hanger covers
- director's chair back
- drapery tiebacks
- footstool

- jewellery box cover
- luggage tag
- notecards
- piano bench cushion
- scrapbook cover
- tissue box cover
- travelling sewing kit
- wastebasket cover

- bell pull
- bookends
- brick doorstop
- Christmas tree ornaments
- collars and cuffs
- dog or cat collar
- fireplace screen
- game board (chess, backgammon)

- key chain
- napkin rings
- pen or pencil case
- picture or mirror frame
- screen divider
- toaster cover
- typewriter cover

- belt
- bookmark
- button covers
- cigarette case
- dice shaker
- dolls
- flask case
- hatband

- lamp shade
- needlebook cover
- phonebook cover
- purse
- tennis racket cover
- tote bag
- wallet

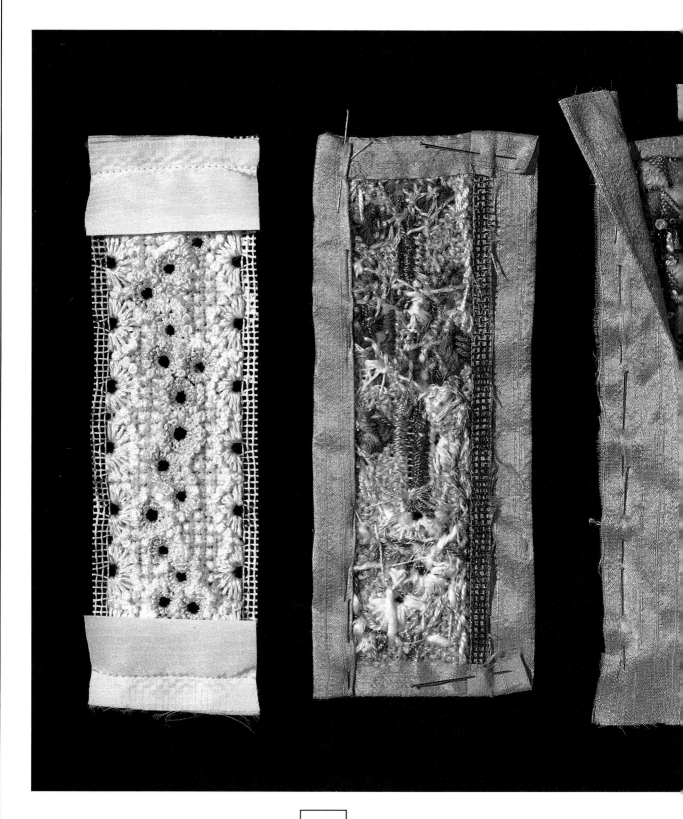

7

MOUNTING AND MAKING UP

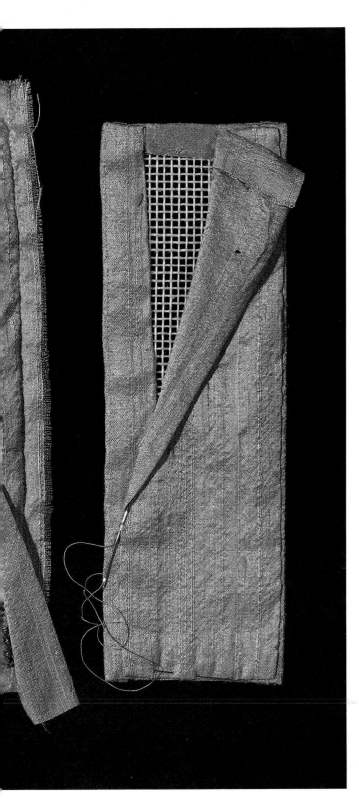

Prior to making up a project thought needs to be given to the alternatives available for obtaining the best possible finish. Constraints such as the availability of time and materials must be taken into consideration.

Even though this is often difficult if not seemingly impossible to achieve, I recommend that mounting and making up be undertaken when there is peace and quiet. One often tends to embark on this procedure while doing three other tasks at the same time. But this is a delicate business, and unnecessary distractions can well lead to mistakes and great frustrations. When the finishing off is done during a quiet period especially set aside for this purpose, those frustrations seem to be fewer. Another way I've found for finishing off my work when I don't seem to have enough time to set aside for completion at one sitting is to make a 'Do List'. I break up the process into very small parts and number each part. For example:

1. Measure and mark seam allowance
2. Cut out seam allowance
3. Overlock seam allowance
4. Buy lining material
5. Cut out wadding

As I complete each part at my convenience, without the worry of planning inside my head because it's all down on paper for me, I tick off each completed task. I have found this a very successful and rewarding procedure.

Straightening the Canvas

Canvas work embroidery sometimes needs straightening or stretching before it can be mounted, particularly when a lot of tent or eyelet stitches have been used. However, this is not always the case if the canvas has been carefully and firmly tensioned on the frame during mounting and working. Also, if the finished work is only slightly distorted, it is possible to pull it into shape when lacing the work to the mounting board.

If you do need to straighten the work, here is the procedure to follow:

1. Cover a board with an old sheet or piece of fabric, or place a piece of white blotting paper on top of the board. With a set square (to ensure properly angled corners), draw the finished shape on to the blotting paper or fabric.

2. Place drawing pins along two opposite sides, starting from the centre point of each side and working towards the corners. The right side of the canvas should be facing down.

3. Stretch and pin the other two sides in the same way. If you have difficulty, sprinkle a little water on the back of the work to assist the stretching process. Take care, however, with canvas which contains a lot of size or stiffening as too much water will make it go limp and puffy.

4. After pinning the distorted canvas to the stretching board, if necessary, prepare a mixture of one part aquadhere or latex wallpaper glue to four parts water. Apply the mixture to the back of the work with a stiff brush, such as a toothbrush. Leave the canvas

pinned to the board for *at least* twenty-four hours, or until it is quite dry.

When a piece of work refuses to stay in shape, particularly when it cannot be mounted over a board as in the case of a cushion or bag, it will be necessary to take such measures.

Mounting and Making Up a Wall Panel

CUTTING OUT THE BACK BOARDS

As mentioned in Chapter 4 on Design, it is easier to design a wall panel working backwards from the size of the finished panel. For those who wish to save time and effort mounting the work, it is an excellent idea to purchase lightweight acid-free masonite cut in standard sizes. Buy one board for the work to be mounted on and a larger one for the backboard.

If you have not done the above and wish to cut out mounting boards to your individual specifications, buy a sheet of lightweight masonite from your local framer or hardware shop. Measure the size carefully, making sure to use a set square to obtain perfect right-angled corners.

Either do it yourself or co-opt a handyperson to saw the masonite to size. Carefully sand the edges for a smooth finish. It is important then to round off the corners with sandpaper. Also, sand the back of each corner to make it thinner. This allows the canvas material to fit better when mitring the corners, making them less bulky.

PREPARING THE CANVAS FOR MOUNTING

1. Straighten the canvas as necessary.

2. Cut out the canvas allowing a seam allowance all around the embroidery of 1 ½ in. to 4 in. (4 to 10 cm), depending on the size of the panel. Overlock the edge with two rows of zig-zag or serpentine stitch on the machine.

Centring the top (front) and bottom (back) mounting boards

1. Measure and draw a horizontal cross A-B-C-D at the centre of the top mounting boards. See Figure 1.

2. On both top and bottom mounting boards draw two horizontal lines parallel to and at an equal distance above and below C-D, forming E-F and G-H. These measurements should be the same on the bottom mounting board as on the top mounting board.

3. On both bottom and top mounting boards draw two vertical lines parallel and at an equal distance from A-B, forming I-J and K-L.

4. The rectangle or square M-N-O-P should measure exactly the same on the bottom mounting board as the top.

5. With a hammer and large nail make holes in both mounting boards at M,N,O and P. Sand them back.

6. Lace firm string lengths, two through M-N and one through O-P, on the top mounting board only.

7. The boards are now ready for lacing, gluing and mounting the fabrics and finishing off the corners and the back.

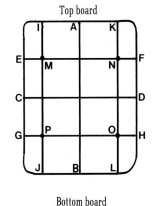

Top board

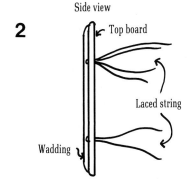

Side view

2

Top board

Laced string

Wadding

1

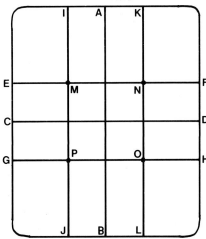

Bottom board

3

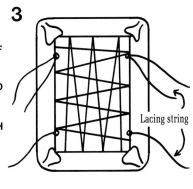

Lacing string

LACING, GLUING AND MOUNTING FABRIC TO THE TOP (FRONT) MOUNTING BOARDS

1. Glue a thin piece of wadding on to the top mounting board (on top of the previously laced string). Trim the edges with a sharp pair of scissors. Refer to Figure 2.

2. Lace the canvas to the top mounting board with unbreakable string or bri-nylon thread, ensuring that the lacing stitches are no more than 1 in. (2.5 cm) apart. Use an unbroken lacing thread; that is do not cut the lacing thread off the ball or skein of thread until the lacing has been completed. Refer to Figure 3.

3. Pull the lacing thread firmly and finish off with several straight stitches.

4. Mitre the corners.

4

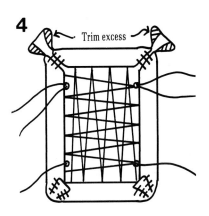

Trim excess

MITRING CORNERS

1. With a sharp pair of scissors cut the canvas ¼ in. to ½ in. (6 to 12 mm) from the corners, forming a forty-five degree angle to the corner. Refer to Figure 4. A triangle of canvas will form at each corner.

2. Sew each corner with large stitches, using double machine thread.

3. Trim each triangle so that there are no hems to turn under.

4. Pull the triangular flap over the join (seam) at each corner, sewing it down with large stitches using doubled machine thread.

5. Finish off the canvas edge that shows on the sides of the top (front) mount.

FINISHING OFF THE CANVAS EDGE

As you will see, an edge of unworked canvas now remains around the edge of the top (front) mount. Using a contrasting or matching thread, straight satin stitch (or gobelin stitch) around the edge of the top mount, ensuring that the thread is thick enough to cover the canvas. If desired, the same colour need not be used to finish off the edge of different areas of your work.

LACING, GLUING AND MOUNTING FABRIC TO THE BOTTOM (BACK) MOUNTING BOARD

Lace a piece of fabric over the bottom mounting board, mitring the corners. It is often but not always desirable to first glue or lace a piece of calico or old sheeting to the backboard, and then lace the matching fabric. This minimises puckering and allows a thin fabric to sit better. This procedure is not necessary for heavier curtain fabrics or velvet.

JOINING TOP AND BOTTOM MOUNTING BOARDS

1. Lace the string from the top mounting board through the holes of the bottom mounting board. Tie two sets of string firmly, leaving loose the strings for the hanging cord. Refer to Figure 5.

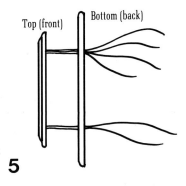

Top (front)   Bottom (back)

5

2. If the top and bottom mounting boards are not tied together tightly enough, lace and tie the two sets of tied strings together with another thread. Refer to Figure 6.

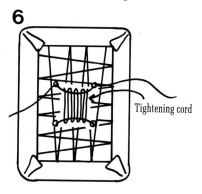

Tightening cord

6

3. Cut out a piece of fabric the same size as the bottom mounting board. Press the edge in ½ in. (12 mm). Pin the fabric to the bottom (back) mounting board. Thread the top lacing (or hanging) strings through this fabric. Glue down the edges with colourless fabric glue.

4. Tie off the loose strings at the top to form the hanging cord. Buttonhole the ends of the string along the cord to finish off the ends and make a firm hanging cord. Refer to Figure 7.

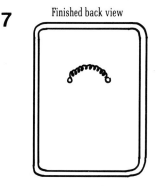

Finished back view

7

ALTERNATIVE HANGING METHOD

Another way to attach the top and bottom mounting boards is to first attach two rings at the back of the bottom mounting board with contact adhesive gel and strong binding tape. Refer to Figure 8. These rings and tapes should be glued on *before* fabric is laced to the board.

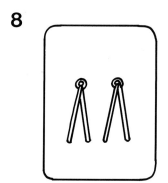

8

1. Attach the top mounting board to the back mounting board, ensuring by measuring first that all sides are even and straight.

2. Cut out a piece of fabric the same size as the bottom mounting board. Press the edge in ¼ in. (6 mm).

3. Cut out two slits to allow the rings to come through. Overlock the edges of the slits.

4. Pin the fabric to the back of the mounting board. Glue down the edge with colourless fabric glue.

5. Attach a hanging cord between the two rings.

Featherweight or Foamboard Mounting

It is now possible to buy featherweight or foamboard from art suppliers or framers, either in a large sheet or cut to size. When cutting foamboard for yourself, always use a very sharp blade in the cutting knife and score it several times rather than pressuring the board with one hard stroke.

Recessed Mounting or Picture Frame Method

This is a very effective way of mounting canvas work and can be adapted equally well to making up and mounting a wall panel, a notebook cover, a photo frame or a mirror surround. Use lightweight masonite or cardboard ¼ in. (6 mm) thick for the bottom mount, and thick cardboard for the top mount.

PREPARING THE BOTTOM MOUNT

1. Cut the board to size. If needed, make two holes for the hanging cord to go through.

2. Cut out a piece of fabric with a 1 in. (2.5 cm) seam allowance. Glue the fabric to the cardboard with colourless fabric glue, mitring the corners. In this instance it is not necessary to sew the mitred corners; careful gluing is very satisfactory.

3. Thread the hanging cord through the holes, if hanging is required. Refer to Figure 9.

PREPARING THE TOP MOUNT

1. Cut a piece of heavy card-

9

Back View
Bottom (back) mount

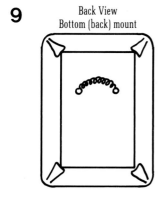

board the same size as the bottom mounting board.

2. Draw four lines, A-B, C-D, E-F, G-H parallel to each side, the desired width of the frame.

3. Curve off each corner. Refer to Figure 10.

10

Back View
Top (front) mount

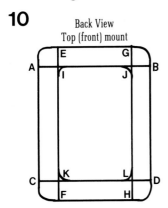

4. Carefully cut out this centre piece with a sharp Stanley knife or other appropriate sharp cutting instrument.

5. Cut out a thin piece of wadding and glue it to the cardboard. If the wadding is too thick tear it apart and use half the thickness.

6. With a sharp pair of scissors trim the edges of the wadding around the inner edge of the frame, as well as around the outer edge.

7. Cut out the mounting fabric (the same fabric as the bottom mount) with a 1 in. (2.5 cm) seam allowance.

8. Glue the mounting fabric with colourless fabric glue to

the cardboard, covering the wadding. Mitre the corners once again with glue. Refer to Figure 11.

11

Back View
Top (front) mount

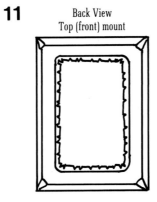

9. Draw a line with a pencil or pen on the fabric ½ in. (12 mm) in from the edge of the hole I-J-K-L. Refer to Figure 11.

10. Snip the fabric at intervals. More snips will be required at the corners.

11. Apply colourless fabric glue in sections around the edge of the hole, gently pulling the fabric back over the edge and gluing to the cardboard. Refer to Figure 12.

12

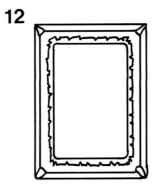

12. Apply glue for ½ in. (12 mm) on top of the just completed edge. Be careful not to apply too much glue close to the edge as it could squeeze through to the front and make an indelible mark.

13. With the fingers, gently press the edge of the embroidery onto the glue area. Ensure that it is centred in the frame

and that seam allowances are concealed.

14. Glue the top and bottom mounts together around the edges.

Cylinders

1. Measure the cylinder to be covered, allowing an extra ¾ in. to 1 ¼ in. (2 to 3 cm) on the width to go round the cylinder as the padding formed by the build-up of thread on the back of the canvas brings the canvas away from the surface of the cylinder, thereby creating a larger area to be covered.

2. Plan ahead for the stitches to be worked where the two edges will meet. It is easier to join stitches at the edges that are different, than areas of stitches which are the same on both sides of the join. For example, a vertical row of ray stitch, cushion or Rhodes stitch could be worked at the join, although it is suggested that the whole vertical row not be of the same stitch as this would draw attention to the join. On the other side of the join almost any other stitch could be worked. The way to overcome this problem is to close the gap with a bridged join. Refer to Figure 15 illustrating the bridged join.

3. In mounting canvas work to a cylinder, you may decide to pad between the canvas and the mount. This can be done using a filling such as polyester wadding, lightly gluing the wadding to the mount with colourless fabric adhesive.

4. To make the join the following alternative methods may be used:

METHOD A

1. Zigzag edges by machine to overlock the join, staggering the rows on top of each other.

2. Fold back the seam allowance for an open seam at the join. The suggested seam allowance is ½ in. (12 mm). Ladder stitch the join. Refer to Figure 13.

13

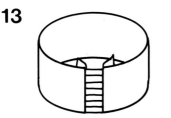

Joining seams for a cylinder using the ladder stitch

14

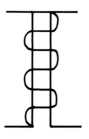

LADDER STITCH

Ladder stitch is an appliqué stitch that produces a concealed join. This is created by the nature of the stitch, which causes the fabric at the join to roll a little thereby concealing the stitches. The reason it is called ladder stitch is because it resembles a ladder when the seams are apart.

Bring the thread out at the corner of the left-hand seam and take the needle through the right-hand seam corner, making a small running stitch approximately ⅛ in. to ¼ in. (3 to 4 mm) long on the seam line. Bring the thread out and take the next running stitch into the left-hand seam making another stitch of the same length exactly on the seam line. Continue taking running stitches, alternately in each join, for about 1 in. (2.5 cm), then firmly pull the thread so that the join closes. Continue working in this manner until the seam is completely joined, finishing off in the corner at

the end of the seam. It is very important to note that each ladder stitch bridging the seam should form a right angle to the seam, as shown in Figure 13, otherwise the stitches will show.

METHOD B

The second alternative is to finish the join with a ribbon or binding. Overlap the two raw canvas seam-allowance edges, which can be ½ in. (12 mm) or more. Tack them together with sewing thread. Appliqué ribbon or binding over the seam allowance to cover the tacking.

METHOD C

Cut off the canvas to the very edge of the area to be worked. This would be done when all the canvas has been embroidered except for a band along the joins, and after the work has been taken off the frame. Cut a strip of canvas 1 in. (2.5 cm) wide by the length of the join, plus a small allowance at each end. Butt the two cut ends together and layer the canvas bridge on to the back of the butted ends, matching the holes.

Secure them in place with pins and a tacking stitch of doubled machine thread. Work canvas stitches over this join, pulling out the tacking thread as you go and it is no longer required. Refer to Figure 15.

15

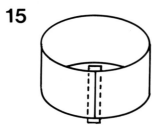

FINISHING THE TOP AND BOTTOM EDGES OF THE CYLINDER

Fold over the overlocked seam allowance of ½ in. (12 mm) at the edge of the embroidery, both at the top and bottom of the cylinder. With a matching thread, join the lid and base to the sides of the cylinder using a ladder stitch (see Figure 13). If the edge still shows unworked canvas, either work stitches over it, apply a twisted cord or work a row of double or Palestrina knots in an appropriate thread. Alternately, work an overcast seam.

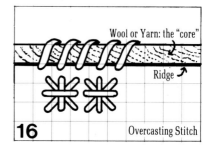

Wool or Yarn: the "core"

Ridge

16 Overcasting Stitch

OVERCAST SEAM

The overcast seam works very well on a curved edge. Here are the instructions:

1. Fold a seam allowance of ¾ in. (2 cm) at the edge of the embroidered canvas to form a fold or ridge, as in the binding stitch. Allow two threads of mono canvas to form the ridge, and one row of double or Penelope canvas.

2. Lay a thread of thick rug yarn, 12-ply knitting yarn or 8-ply knitting yarn doubled along the ridge to create a core. This also prevents the canvas from showing.

3. Using a matching or contrasting thread, overcast a stitch into each hole of the canvas, as shown in Figure 16. Stitching can also be taken to the second row of embroidery as well as the first, in which case it would be best to work a row of tent stitch as the last row before the seam allowance.

BINDING STITCH

This stitch may also be used for finishing off edges. It is especially suitable for small projects, boxes and cylinders. Work the binding stitch around the top and bottom of the cylinder and around the edges of the lid and base. Sew the joins together with ordinary sewing thread that will not show between the binding stitches.

The binding stitch is illustrated in colour on page *xiii*.

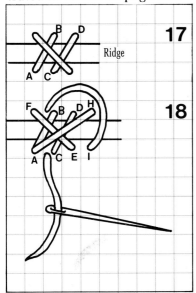

1. Fold back ¾ in. (2 cm) of canvas, with the fold being right at the edge of the embroidered canvas. In the case of mono canvas allow two threads to form the fold or ridge. For double or Penelope canvas, one row of threads forms the fold or ridge.
2. Bring the thread out at A, the beginning of the edge facing towards you. Work two overcasting stitches into two consecutive holes from left to right (A-B-C-D).
3. Bring the thread back over the ridge to the first stitch at the beginning, that is to A.
4. Go forward three threads to the right and over the ridge and insert the needle at the back, A-H, coming out at the front at I.
5. Go back two threads to the left at B and over the ridge and insert the needle at the back at B, coming out at the front at C.
6. Continue this herringbone rhythm forward three threads, back two threads, backwards and forwards over the ridge of canvas.

If a lining is required it can be brought right up to the edge of the binding stitch and sewn into place with a hemming

stitch using sewing thread, forming a neat finish.

When selecting a thread to work the binding stitch you must consider the desired effect. A thick wool will produce a corded, thick ridge. Coton perle, No. 5 crochet cotton and other similar threads will give a finer edge. Alternately, stranded cotton or metallic threads can be quite distinctive when used on a narrower edge. It is wise to experiment with different effects on scraps of canvas using different threads, and then choose the best effect for the purpose you require.

WORKING THE LID AND BASE

To make a lid to fit the top of the cylinder:

1. Carefully measure the diameter of the circle at the top of the cylinder *after* the canvas has been mounted around the cylinder. Draw a circle onto ordinary writing paper, cut it out, and use this as a pattern to check the correct size of the lid. If the lid is to be detachable, allowances should be made for this when measuring the diameter. Cut out a piece of very firm cardboard according to the correct pattern size.
2. The lid of the box may be worked in canvas embroidery, or can simply be made out of a matching coloured fabric. The base of the cylinder can also be covered with a matching coloured fabric — this will depend on the purpose and intended use of the cylinder, whether it is to stand vertically or horizontally, and whether the base will be seen.
3. Cover the round shape of the lid and base and leave a

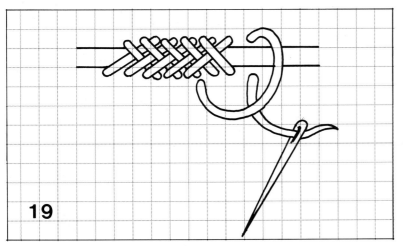

seam allowance of ¾ in. (2 cm), which should be overlocked by machine. If overlocking canvas, do so by using machine zigzag stitches, staggering two or three rows on top of each other.

20

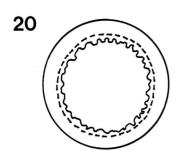

4. Make a gathering stitch ½ in. (12 mm) in from the edge of the seam allowance. Refer to Figure 20. Use ordinary sewing thread, doubled, for gathering fabric and a thicker thread (such as No. 5 crochet cotton) for gathering canvas. Overlap the first few gathering stitches for about 1 in. (2.5 cm), place the round cardboard lid on the back of the fabric or canvas and pull the gathering stitches firmly. Tie off the gathering thread. Join to the cylinder.

5. If the lid is detachable cut out a round piece of medium-weight cardboard slightly smaller than the top piece and cover with a matching fabric. Sandwich the two circles together with clear fabric glue.
6. If desired, trim the edge of the lid with a twisted cord or reverse Palestrina knot.
7. To finish off the lid of the cylinder you might use a buttonholed ring or a large attractive bead attached to the lid, by which it can be lifted off the cylinder. Refer to Chapter 8 on Finishing Touches.

8

FINISHING TOUCHES

*N*o book on embroidery would be complete without a chapter on finishing touches and trimmings. Ever since people have been doing handwork, the most fascinating decorations have been made using fabric, needle and threads. I find the greatest pleasure in adding the finishing touches, the 'icing on the cake'. Even a beautiful embroidery is transformed by the addition of tassels, cords, binding, fringes and buttonholed rings and loops.

I include here instructions on how to make all of these. Through the choice of different threads and yarns you will become ingenious at inventing variations to these ideas. You'll find that the flair of these trimmings will affect the overall impression of your embroidery, making it seem utilitarian, bright, rich, exotic or colourful. Try as many of them as you can. If you can spare any of these ornaments, put them in your reference folder for memory's sake.

Tassels

Tassels are a lot of fun to make as well as being a very attractive finishing touch. They can decorate a box lid, the bottom of a bookmark or a needle case. They can be attached to cords and used as a book mark for folders, cushion corners, key rings, scissor tags and wall panels.

The easiest method I have discovered to make tassels is as follows:

1. Cut a piece of firm card into a rectangle the desired length of the tassel. Refer to Figure 1.

1

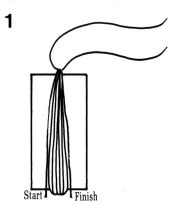

Start　Finish

2. Using the chosen thread, wind it round and round the cardboard until there is a sufficient bulk of thread to make a good tassel in proportion to the weight of the thread, starting and finishing the thread at the bottom of the card. *Note:* when winding the thread around the card, build up the thread on top of itself at the top of the head of the tassel so that it is as narrow as possible. This makes it easier to proceed to the next step.

3. Cut a length of the same thread about 18 in. (45 cm) long and thread it with a needle under the wound thread at the top of the tassel, tying it with a firm double knot.

4. Take the circle of thread off the cardboard; do not cut the end at this stage. Cut another length of thread approximately 8 in. (20 cm) long and tie it around the threads using a firm double knot at the distance from the top of the tassel where you wish the tassel head to finish.

2

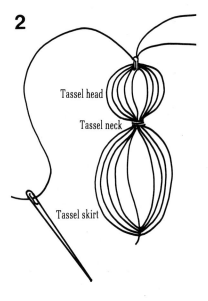

Tassel head

Tassel neck

Tassel skirt

This becomes the 'neck'. Refer to Figure 2. Let the ties blend with the threads of the tassel skirt and trim any excess so it doesn't get in the way whilst sewing the tassel head. Cut a long piece of thread and thread it into a tapestry needle. It is best if the tassel head is embroidered without starting a new thread in the process. Thread the needle up through the centre of the tassel skirt and head, leaving the tail of the thread hanging loose to blend with the other threads in the skirt. Again, refer to Figure 2.

5. The tassel head is now ready to be embroidered. Using detached buttonhole stitch, start at the top and work in a spiral down to the tassel neck. The most difficult

part is to start the detached buttonhole stitches; if the following instructions are followed it shouldn't be too difficult:

3

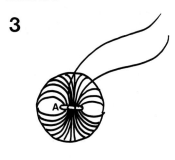

4

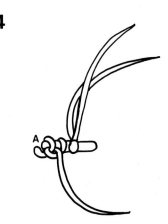

5

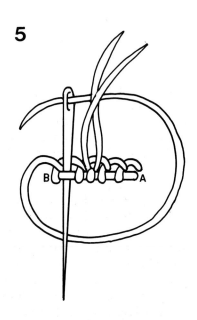

6. Looking down at the top of the tassel, as shown in Figure 3, is the bar that ties the top of the tassel. Bring thread out at A (as seen in Figure 3) and work two detached buttonhole stitches around the bar at the left of the knot, then two more detached buttonhole stitches on the bar on the right side of the knot. Turn the tassel around and take a detached buttonhole stitch at B, between the previous stitch and around the bar. Take another stitch around the bar on the left-hand side of the knot and two further stitches on the bar to the right-hand side of the knot. This takes you back to A. Continue taking detached buttonhole stitches in the previous row, going round and round in a spiral. Care needs to be taken with the tension of each stitch so that it is neither too tight nor too loose; only practice will teach you the correct amount of tension. Very tight tension produces a narrow, thin tassel head whilst too little tension results in a baggy, loose tassel head.

7. If a tassel head doesn't turn out the way you planned or desire, don't throw it away. Cover it with needleweaving, beads, or in any other decorative manner and you will be surprised at the result.

8. When you have detached buttonhole stitched to about three-quarters of the way down the tassel head, finish off the head by stitching through the head at the neck. That is, for every detached buttonhole stitch taken into the previous row, at the same time pass the needle under the neck thread pulling gently but firmly so that the mesh created by the detached buttonhole stitches spreads evenly to cover the head. See Figure 7.

6

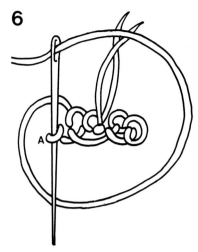

7

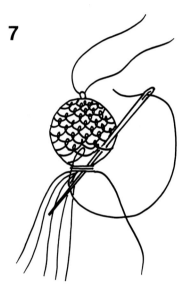

9. Finish off the remaining thread by passing it through the padding of the head and then down again through the middle of the tassel, trimming it off to the same length as the tassel skirt.

10. With a sharp pair of scissors cut the bottom loop of the tassel to form a straight even end. Don't trim the ends too much as this can prove disastrous, the skirt of the tassel ending up too short.

11. Attach the tassel to a twisted cord, or buttonhole stitch the ties at the top of the head to finish off.

Different sorts of tassels can be produced by experimentation, changing the proportion of the head, neck and skirt. It is very important that the various parts of the tassel are proportionate to each other, to the tassel as a whole and to the article that it will decorate.

Twisted Cord

1. Cut a thread six times the length of the required finished cord. That is, for the finished cord to measure 12 in. (30 cm) cut a length of thread 6 feet (180 cm) long.

2. Fold the 6 foot length of thread in half and place the half-way loop over a hook or doorknob.

3. Twist the ends of the thread between the fingers until it is twisted very tightly.

4. Place one finger at a point half-way along the cord and fold the cord so that the ends are together. To prevent unwanted looping on the cord, twist the cord first along its length to aid the twisting process before releasing the folded end, allowing the cord to form its own natural twist.

5. Knot the ends together with a knot.

8

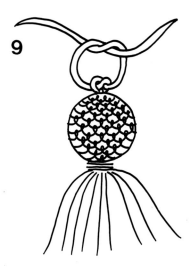

9

Tied Cord

1. Cut two lengths of thread and knot two ends together.
2. Using the two ends of the thread keep on tying knots one after the other, one on top of the other until the cord is the required length. This is an attractive cord that is very easy to make.

Binding with Fabric

One method of finishing off small projects such as cushions and bookmarks is to bind them with fabric.

1. Cut out a suitable matching strip of fabric longer than the required length to be bound. The width should be double the required width plus seam allowance.
2. Fold the fabric in half lengthwise. This becomes the binding strip.
3. Pin the binding to the opposite ends of the article and on the front, right sides together, with a seam allowance ¼ in. (6 mm) from the edge.
4. Machine stitch the binding strip to the article.
5. Fold the binding strip to the back and sew the folded edge to the machine stitched seam,

using a small hand-hemmed stitch.
6. Pin the binding strip to the remaining two sides and on the front of the article, allowing an extra ½ in. (12 mm) at each end of the binding strip.

Finishing off a bookmark is shown in colour on page v
7. Machine stitch the binding strip with a seam allowance ¼ in. (6 mm) from the edge.
8. Fold back the ends of the strips.
9. Fold the binding strip to the back and sew the folded edge to the machine-stitched line using a small hand-hemmed stitch.
10. To line the back of the bookmark, stitch a piece of matching fabric with edges turned to the inside held in place with a small hand-hemmed stitch.

Fringes

Velvet stitch or Ghiordes knot are ideal for working on the edge of an article for fringeing. Alternatively, lengths of evenly cut threads can be pulled through each hole with the aid of a crochet hook and knotted.

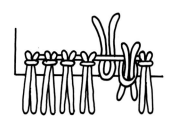

Buttonholed Covered Rings

Covered rings and washers have many uses: a handle for a cylinder lid, handles through which to lace rouleaux ties at the top of a purse or bag, decoration for embroidery panels

on which to create another layer of texture, decoration of tassel heads, linked collection to form a chain belt or design units within needleweaving.

Using various sizes of metal curtain rings or metal washers, buttonhole stitch around them with any kind of suitable thread. Plastic curtain rings are very practical and have an added advantage in that they can be washed, provided the thread and embroidery are also washable. The buttonhole stitch creates a small hole at the edge where the loop is formed and it is sometimes necessary to work twice around the ring for a better cover, depending on the thread used.

FINGER RINGS OR BUTTONHOLED LOOPS
If you don't have any rings or wish to make soft covered rings, first wind the thread several times around your thumb or fingers depending on the desired size. Buttonhole stitch the circled threads, which will form the core of the ring. Smaller rings can be wound and buttonholed around a pencil.

Beautiful effects can be created by applying the soft rings to embroidery as circles, or twisting them first into different shapes and then applying them to the embroidery. Canvas work and surface stitches can then be worked within the circle and in the spaces in between them. Interesting textured effects can be created by using eyelet stitch, French or bullion knots combined with beads.

See colour illustration depicting buttonholed loops on page viii.

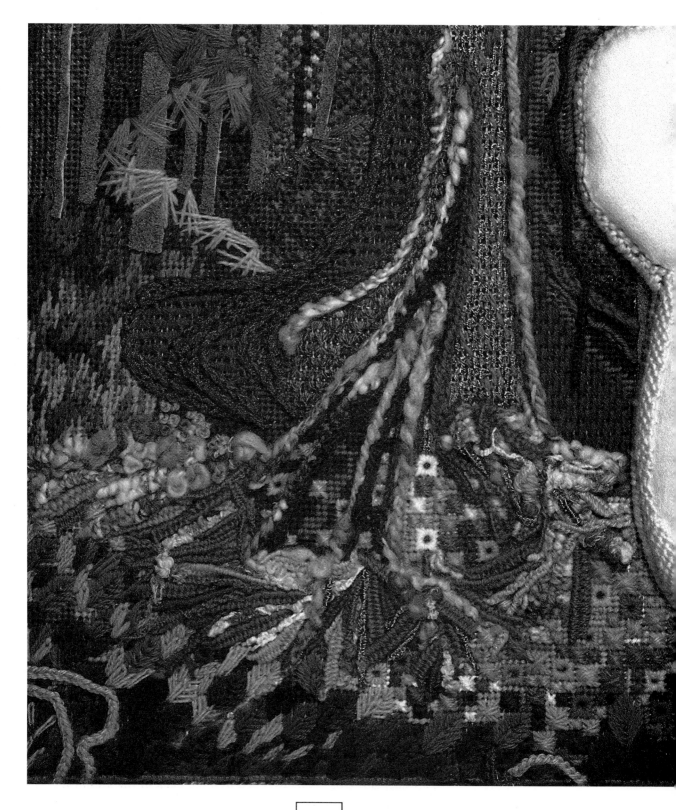

9

ONE LAST WORD

s one last suggestion I offer to you a checklist that I find helpful always to keep handy:

1. Spend time planning the design.

2. Although it is nice to have the approval of family and friends, do not be deterred by uninformed remarks about your embroidery. For example, you might be creating a delightful garden scene when half-way through the project a passing comment like 'That looks just like a hippopotamus' comes from some passer-by. Even *you* should defer judgment of the work until it is complete! Most often it is in the final throes of finishing an embroidery project that final touches and additions draw together the piece as a whole.

3. If it is necessary to work when you are tired, choose procedures that are automatic and require little thought. This will prevent unpicking later.

4. Maintain an even tension in the thread.

5. Always use a straight rust-free needle.

6. When using tapestry and crewel wools, test the wool to ensure that the needle is threaded correctly. That is, hold the thread in good light and draw it between your finger and thumb. In one direction you will see that the fibres are more obvious. When pulled in the other direction the fibres lay down onto the wool. This is the way the thread should be pulled through the canvas for a better result as there is not the irritation of pulling the wool 'against the grain'.

7. Ensure that the strands of wool are not twisted, and that they are kept side by side on the canvas, particularly when using crewel wool, thus preventing a 'thinning' and uneven texture.

8. Start your embroidery with a knot at the front within the area being worked, about 2 in. (5 cm) away from where the stitches are to commence. Alternatively, start with a knot at the back of the work, make a couple of back stitches to anchor the thread, snip off the knot and bring the working thread out to the front of the canvas.

9. Finish off by slipping the thread backward and forward into the back of the stitches.

10. Use a thread that is not too long. Some twisted thread such as wool crêpe will need to be used in shorter lengths as the twist unravels after a while, producing an uneven texture.

11. Always use sharp embroidery scissors to cut threads.

12. When using double thread ensure that two single threads are cut and threaded together in the same direction through the needle. If a single thread is threaded through the needle once and doubled back for extra thickness, the fibres and natural twist will pull in different directions.

Finally, think of these elements as the main ingredients for creative embroiderers:
- stimulation
- inspiration
- imagination
- enthusiasm
- information — a thorough knowledge of the techniques of canvas embroidery.

As in all things, stimulation is a basic ingredient, and a very important one. Too often it is thought to be something that 'just happens' to those people 'lucky' enough to be creative. But such stimulation is something that needs to be consciously planned and worked at.

Inspiration is a quality that can be nurtured and developed by following suggestions like those in Chapter 4 on Design. It comes from beholding beautiful colours and threads. Inspiration also comes from sharing your ideas with other embroiderers and artists.

Imagination is triggered and spurred on by enthusiasm. Maintain your enthusiasm and open up your interest and awareness in the beauty around you. And the more technique you can learn, the more 'food' for your imagination!

EMBROIDERERS' GUILDS

United Kingdom
Embroiderers' Guild,
Apart. 41, Hampton Court Palace,
EAST MOLESEY, Surrey
KT8 9AU

Centre for Embroidery,
Fashion and Textile Studies
66 New Bond St
LONDON W1Y 9DF

United States
The Embroiderers' Guild of
America,
200 Fourth Ave.,
Louisville
KENTUCKY 40202

Canada
Embroiderers' Association of
Canada Inc.,
P.O. Box 541
Station B
LONDON ONTARIO
N6A 4WI

Australia
The Embroiderers' Guild, NSW
Inc.
76 Queen Street,
CONCORD WEST NSW 2138
Tel: 02 743 2501

The Embroiderers' Guild, Victoria
170 Wattletree Road,
MALVERN VIC 3144
Tel: 03 509 2222

The Embroiderers' Guild, A.C.T.,
G.P.O. Box 146,
CANBERRA A.C.T. 2601
Tel: 062 49 6542

The Embroiderers' Guild Qld. Inc.
149 Brunswick Street,
P.O. Box 150,
FORTITUDE VALLEY QLD 4006
Tel: 07 252 8629

The Embroiderers' Guild S.A. Inc.
16 Hughes Street,
MILE END S.A. 5031
Tel: 08 234 1104

The Embroiderers' Guild of
Tasmania, Inc.
P.O. Box 158,
LAUNCESTON TAS. 7250

Hobart Embroiderers' Guild,
P.O. Box 387,
SANDY BAY TAS. 7005

The Embroiderers' Guild of
Western Australia (Inc.)
8/80 Peninsula Road
MAYLANDS WA 6051

New Zealand
Association of New Zealand
Embroiderers' Guilds Inc.
Kathleen Owens (Secretary)
P.O. Box 348
PARAPARAUMU

GLOSSARY OF TERMS

Anchoring stitch — two or more back stitches normally worked at the back of the embroidery to hold the thread in place

Back stitch — a stitch which goes back and touches the previous stitch and in appearance resembles the straight stitch formed by a sewing machine

Bias binding or Bias tape — a strip of fabric cut on the true bias with the edges ironed in, prepared for sewing onto a raw edge and is used instead of straight tape as it will stretch around curves

Cotton tape — woven cotton ribbon usually found in haberdashery or notions counters

Hem stitch — a small stitch taken alternately through two fabrics to hold them together

Overlock — stitching over a raw edge of fabric with machine stitching to prevent fraying of the fabric

Oversew (or topsew) — a small even stitch sewn over the raw edge of fabric

Perforations — holes made by piercing, a series of punched holes. In needlepoint embroidery the holes formed between stitch units

Primary pattern — the pattern created by needlepoint stitches

Secondary pattern — the pattern created by the perforations of the primary pattern of stitches

Selvedge — the edge of a woven cloth

Serpentine stitch — a series of back stitches, usually a machine stitch, forming a wavy line, often used for overlocking raw edges of fabric

Stab stitch — inserting the needle from the front to the back or from the back to the front, then pulling the thread through before proceeding to the next stitch. Do not take the needle through the fabric more than once before pulling the thread through as this distorts the fabric and creates puckering

Stiletto — a very sharp pointed instrument used for making holes in fabric

Waste knot — a knot tied on the end of a thread which is used to anchor the sewing thread and then snipped off

Whip stitch — similar to oversewn stitch, refers to a small, even stitch sewn over a previous line of stitching or a rolled edge of fabric

INDEX OF STITCHES